MW00874123

I Ran Away to Mexico

Mexico

An Unexpected Spiritual Journey

Blessings —
Laura

Laura LaBrie

Copyright © 2016 Laura LaBrie

All rights reserved.

ISBN: **1539529770**
ISBN-13: **978-1539529774**

DEDICATION

For Lee because he was with me every step of the way and for my children Sarah, Michael, and Thomas for supporting their mother's crazy journey.

CONTENTS

DON'T COME HERE TO HELP US

Come live with us.

MEXICO

1. IF ONLY

My heart is still broken. When I allow my conscious mind access to what is deep inside, I can still feel it. When I quiet myself, I feel the pain, the loneliness I am trying to cover up with life, with adventures, with volunteering, with wine, with friends. It is still there, underlying everything I do. It prevents me from getting in touch with myself, from slowing down and hearing my own heart. It is very deep and colors everything dark purple. How I long to be free from this pain. If I cannot heal, I will never be free. I will need to cover up my interior, to hide from myself, to disconnect. And how can I ever be whole if I am disconnected from myself?

I have been running. I know this. Of course, I have experienced many amazing things and I know I have encouraged many people along the way. And maybe this will just be my reality from now on. But I feel there must be a settled place, a place where I feel good again. I am driving myself into the ground, with no recourse, and I see the end of this road is not a good one. How do I escape from it? How do I find a road that is paved with life, not destruction?

I feel I must make a change, but I am afraid to do it.

I am afraid to face the pain. But if I don't, I am afraid of the ramifications of that too.

And now I am supposed to write, write about Mr. Sugar and Chicken

Bone and the adventures I have had, which could be great stuff and should be easy to do. But in order to plug into my creative side, I must brush against that pain.

And in the brushing, all I can do is gather my life-force into my breast and hold it there, away from what hurts. All I can do is retreat.

How can I escape from this miserable prison I am in?

And so off I run, doing anything possible to hide from what is inside.

And those who surround me see my life and envy...if only they knew.

2. BLUE PEOPLE

Blue people? Blue people? Are you kidding me?

Darryl was sick. He was taking experimental medication for a brain tumor. The tumor was gone. They had removed it in surgery and it didn't come back, but they insisted he needed to take medication or it would. And anything was preferable to death by brain tumor.

I am sure it was killing him.

Not the tumor. The medication.

He would not get out of bed, even though he was perfectly capable of it. He spit his food at me when I tried to get him to eat. He rambled on about things that made no sense. He said a little girl in a white dress was in the room. He said his brother was sitting in the rocking chair next to him.

All that I could handle, somehow, even though it was devastating to me. At least it seemed within the parameters or normality—for a brain tumor.

But when he told me not to worry because the four blue people would take care of me, I lost it.

I told him I was leaving him. I packed a small bag and drove to the pier— my place of sanctuary. I called a good friend and she talked me down.

4

How could I leave him in this condition? He needed me. He could not take care of himself. After twenty-seven years of marriage, it was my duty to be at his side.

So I went back.

Two weeks later, he died. I won't bore you with the details except to say this, he died in his sleep and I was in his arms.

It wasn't until a year later that I remembered something a pastor friend said to me.

He was in my kitchen long before Darryl even got sick. He told me I had four angels. I asked him to describe them and, in truth, all I remember was that one was female and she was small. I think the others were male, but there was nothing out of the ordinary about the description—at least for angels—because I am sure I would remember it if there had been.

So what did that have to do with blue people?

Well maybe nothing.

But there were four.

I looked up *blue people* online. I found a reference to people with odd bluish skin living in Kentucky.

I didn't think that had much bearing on my question.

I also found a reference to Atlantis. There was a race of blue people— tall, intelligent, blue skinned. Interesting. As I kept looking, I found stories—many stories—of people who saw other-worldly beings with glowing blue skin. In every story, these were good beings who brought wisdom and enlightenment. Hmmm.

I have no answers. Not definitive ones, anyway. But I do know this; Since my husband passed away, I have had help. I like concrete answers, even if they are spiritual ones. But, I know I can't always get them. Or sometimes I have to wait patiently for them to come.

In the meantime, I know there is someone, or *someones* helping me. I see it nearly every day. I think of things I desire and they come to pass. I ask for signs of encouragement and they appear. It's like the universe is aligning itself on my behalf. I do believe in God and I do think He is the Creator of all that we know. But I do not always understand the channels God uses to help us. Some people talk about angels they have seen. Some talk about spirit guides or good energy. Apparently, I have Blue People. And for now, that's ok with me.

3. AKUMAL ASHES

So I ran away to Mexico. I always said I would if things got really bad. My husband and I spent our 25th wedding anniversary there and fell in love with a little fishing village on the Yucatan. So I went back. And I brought him with me.

They almost didn't let me through customs at the airport. They wanted me to open the urn his ashes were in. I suppose they wanted to see if I was smuggling in cocaine (which is stupid because people don't smuggle it from the US into Mexico, it goes the other way) I had all the necessary paper work, but they were suspicious.

The guy checking our luggage said I needed to open the urn, but he didn't want to be the one to look inside. He went to get someone else, who went to get some else, who went to get someone else. Apparently, the Mexicans are very superstitious about the dead. For me, that was a good thing. Finally, I was able to leave the airport with my husband's remains undisturbed.

I went to my favorite little hotel in Puerto Morelos where my good friends, Crescent and William, have their dive shop. I put the urn on the shelf and I left the room and locked it. I sat on the beach all day. I stared at the waves and tried to be social to people who walked by. I was numb.

Two days later, Crescent agreed to go to Akumal with me. Akumal is a beach town with a bay where turtles come every year to lay their eggs. In fact, Akumal means *place of the turtles* in Mayan. The reef there is close to shore. You can swim out and watch tiny, brightly colored fish and sea fans and underwater flying turtles in peace under the hot Mexican sun. It was where my beloved wanted to spend his final days. I promised I would take him there, not for his final days, but for eternity.

It rained.

Still I hired a small panga to take us out to the reef. So we went, Crescent and I. And my daughter. She was the one who kept my head above water.

This is what I wrote later in my journal concerning that day.

Mexico wasn't what I thought it would be. I planned a whale shark adventure, some snorkeling and a trip into the biosphere. Little did I know a storm was brewing.

It was late afternoon on day two of my trip and the thunderheads were gathering. I'd already hired a boat for my trip out to the reef and despite the threatening weather, I was reluctant to cancel. So, I watched the clouds and then the rain.

The ashes were in a beautiful wooden box, in a soft purple drawstring bag, in a dark green fabric shopping bag. I had not looked inside. How could I?

I figured the rain would pass, so I stashed the bag between my feet in the front seat of a dear friend's van and made the 45-minute trip to Akumal Bay.

Ah Akumal, where endangered sea turtles float in the clear Caribbean and sea fans wave in a watery wind fifteen feet beneath the surface of the sea. You were good to me.

Thank you for embracing my dear one and taking him into your depths where he can rest and I can visit him again someday.

The sky was dark and the shore was green. We motored slowly back to the beach and I splashed into the shallows and waded onto the sand.

I am so tired of waxing poetic. Life is what it is. I spent a few moments playing with my friend's three-year-old son and then we headed to the dolphin pools and had dinner. I have no idea what I ate. I suppose, if I thought long enough, I could remember. But what does it matter?

The following day, word came a hurricane was poised to engulf the entire east coast. I made plans to go home and beat the storm.

So long Mexico

I am not sure if I will return.

Little did I know, I would be back sooner than expected. And not only would I be back, but I would make my home there. I would wander those beaches and make lifelong friends in those sleepy fishing villages. I would find comfort and begin to get outside of myself and immerse myself in the beauty around me—the beauty I was meant to somehow document and share—the beauty of the people and the flowers and the families and the food and the lack and the relationships and the heat and the struggle and the grace and the laughter. How do I write it all down? How do I take this thing that is burning inside me and expose it to you?

Mexico set me on a journey like no other. A journey that began with loss and resulted in setting my course, dredging up compassion and passion in me that previously, I barely knew existed.

We never know where life will bring us. We cannot foresee what devastation might bring us into joy.

I buried my husband in Mexico and I found life there. It continues to this day. As you read the rest of my story, I hope you will feel the passion that burns within me, forgive all my wanderings, and try to hear what I am trying to say.

4. DON'T HELP US

"Don't come here to help us."

Funny how a small sentence can change everything.

I came back to Mexico with the intent of teaching English as a second language to little Mayan children. I wanted to do some good in the world and I loved to teach, so it seemed like a good plan.

Until I met Fernando.

I had only been back a few days and I was ping-ponging between desperate desolation and delight. My soul was empty, but I loved the culture and the people of Mexico and I was excited to begin a new adventure. It was better than drinking myself to death on my couch in Virginia, anyway.

One morning when the sun was not yet hot, I went to the market next to the church with the idea of buying some fresh cheese, some chilies, maybe an avocado, and a mango or two. And there was Fernando. He was a small Mexican man, dignified and greying. His English, although heavily accented, was easy to understand. I struck up a conversation with him and poured out all my bubbly good hopes of giving back to the poor Mexican babies, when he very politely and compassionately rocked my world.

"If you want my advice," he offered, "don't come here to help us."

I tried to hide the fact that I needed to pick my jaw up off the cement.

"You Americans come down here with good intentions, but you don't know us. You don't know what we need. If you really want to help us, come live with us. Eventually, you will find where you fit in."

My bubbles all popped. I almost forgot the chilies and cheese. Thoughts spiraled through my head. Fernando was right. Most Americans go to poor countries thinking they have all the answers. But they don't. And in all fairness, how can they?

It's one thing to look at a culture from the outside. From the outside we judge by looking though glasses colored with our own culture. What would it be like to look out from the inside? What would it feel like to let go of my agenda and just *be*. I am such a goal oriented person that it wouldn't be easy. But then again, after the rug was pulled out from under me with the loss of my husband, I didn't really know what I wanted. My world was in turmoil. Goals were easy to think of, but difficult to stick to. The stress of his illness had stolen my logical reasoning and I needed time to just be.

I turned the idea over in my mind. And of course, I went and hung out at the local expat bar and shared a drink and some laughter with the with expat acquaintances I had recently made.

But the idea was there to stay.

And in the end, it changed everything.

5. NOTES ON LIVING IN CENTRAL AMERICA

Central America is a beautiful place. Full of rugged mountains and active volcanoes and steaming rain forests and deserted beaches and remote islands and exotic wild life like monkeys and sloths and jaguars and crocodiles and scarlet macaws and quetzals and incredibly poisonous snakes and tiny, brightly colored frogs and whale sharks and spotted eagle rays and hundreds of miles of coral reefs and... well I could make a ten-page list and I'd still be writing.

The natural resources are abundant. Huge swaths of land are almost untouched by human hands. Indigenous people still live in a fashion close to the way they have lived for thousands of years. Expats flock from all over the world. Shots of tequila and local beers are in grand supply. Small villages offer a real sense of community. Farmers markets are packed with exotic fruits like mammon chino and guanabana and maracuya.

There are big expat communities all through Central America where English is spoken and Facebook groups offer real live support and quick connections in unfamiliar places. In fact, people are arriving in droves, fleeing the robotic lives of first-world countries and looking for something more authentic. They are building homes and starting businesses in small mountain villages and sleepy beach towns. They are learning how to slow down and embrace Latin culture and life, which isn't always easy to do.

I love Central America. I love how connected the people are. I love the town squares and marketplaces where everyone stops and says, "Hi!" and I love the outdoor restaurants where people you have never met sit at your table. I love the mix of people. I know people from South Africa, Israel, Venezuela, Columbia, Argentina, Australia, Germany, Belgium, Aruba, Spain, Italy, India, Norway, England, New Zealand. The list goes on and on. These people are my friends. It's wonderful to have friends from around the world and when they sit down at the table together it makes for some really interesting conversation and brings a sense of how small the world is and how alike we all are. I have never found this back home.

Life is simple here. Well, there are expats who come from the US and Canada and try to bring their country with them, but it never goes over very well. It's easy to come here and think that you can merge your way of living back home with the amazingness of all that is here. But you can't. I have seen it over and over again and I have tried. It just doesn't work. Things are slower, MUCH slower. For example; It took me six weeks to open a bank account in Costa Rica!

Living here means changing.

You come here and see the slow pace of life and the way people chat at the check-out counter at the grocery store and how people take time to have lunch for two hours in the middle of the work day and, if you are here on vacation, that's wonderful. But when you have to get something done because you LIVE here, it gets frustrating. You want to get your wifi hooked up in your new house and you drive a half-hour into town through crazy traffic that includes bicycles carrying bed frames and motorcycles carrying entire families and oxen pulling carts full of palm berries and dogs sleeping in the street and when you finally get there, alive thankfully, the place is closed for lunch. From twelve to two. And its twelve-fifteen.

So you have to learn to adjust.

Some people do and some don't. Many leave before the two-year mark. They can't handle the electricity going out and the inconsistency of the wifi and the slow service at restaurants. But it's OK. They simply aren't happy here and so they go home. It isn't for everyone.

Adjusting to life in Central America means letting go of the need to be in control. It means letting go of the drive to be goal oriented. It means letting go of the need for everything to be done decently and in order. And making that change can be very freeing.

Don't worry, 'bout a ting. 'Cause ever little ting gonna be alright.

We worry so much. We stress over things that seem to hold so much weight. We don't sleep. We are depressed and filled with anxiety. And we are so stuck in that way of life that we cannot see the fullness of it. We feel that things need to change and so we move to a place with a slower lifestyle, but we are so entrenched in our way of living that we feel if we let go of it we will die.

And we will.

But the part of us that will die is that part that was killing us. And if we can allow it to go without too much kicking and screaming, we find we are finally living. We find we can breathe, maybe for the first time since we were children. We find we can belly laugh again. We find ourselves finally relaxing. Like when you didn't even realize you were clenching your teeth and your fists and when you finally let go the muscles hurt because you were holding them that way for so long.

And then life begins to get into a routine. You walk on the beach in the morning and then you stop by your favorite little café and order your favorite coffee. You don't worry about how long it takes them to make the coffee. You strike up a conversation with someone you've never met before and before you know it you are both laughing. And then the coffee comes and you are surprised at how fast it was (even though it took ten minutes) and you walk back out into the sunshine smiling from your eyes.

You drive through the crazy traffic and are amazed at the horse carrying a propane tank and you swerve around the dog sleeping in the sunshine in the middle of the road and you admire the sleeping dog's peace of mind. And when you get to the internet place that's closed for lunch and discover you have an hour and forty-five minutes to wait, you switch gears and head for that little food cart on the corner, the one that has the grilled meat on a stick. You park and get out of your car and you order one and have the Rasta guy slather it in hot sauce. Then you go for a walk and look at all the little shops you always missed before because you were driving past and you savor your snack like it was a lollipop. And you know if there is someone at your house waiting for you to get back, they will wait peacefully, because Latin American culture is like that.

We were putting cable in at our little house in Panama. And just when the guy had finished putting the dish on the roof and they were coming down to go inside and hook everything up, the electricity went out. So they waited for a bit, and when it didn't come back on they made a phone call to see what was going on. They found out that the electric company was doing some work and it would be four to five hours before the power would be turned back on.

So they kicked up their feet and they drank a soda and they chatted with us and taught us some Spanish and they enjoyed the afternoon. They only got paid by how many jobs they did each day, so the fact that they could not finish our job and move on to the next one was going to cost them money. But they didn't mind. Life had offered them the chance to relax and they took it!

As much as I love the natural beauty and exotic feeling of countries like Mexico, Costa Rica, and Panama, it's the ability to slow down and enjoy the little things in life that keeps me here. It's the slowly allowing myself to die to the need to be in control that has made room for unexpected adventures and authentic joys. I am grateful for the change Latin America has demanded of me. It's a change I will carry with me for the rest of my life, no matter where I may go. You can come to the beautiful mountains and beaches of this exotic isthmus thinking you will change your space into what you want it to be. But in the end, my friend, it will have its way with you!

6. MANIFESTING ON STEROIDS

I play the piano. Rather I would say, my life force mixes with that of the vibrations coming from its strings. I am not whole without its expression and thus it is very difficult for me to be away from it.

So, as my time in Mexico lengthened, my discomfort at not having my musical connection increased.

I am not a good guitar player, but I thought maybe I could work on my skill and alleviate some of my distress by practicing on a small guitar.

Of course, I did not know how long I would be in Mexico. So I didn't want to spend much money on a guitar as I might be winging away on an airplane at any time.

But I wanted a good guitar.

I wanted a beautiful, parlor-sized guitar since it has a small neck and I have small hands. And I didn't want to pay more than a hundred dollars for it.

This desire formed in my mind early in the day. I walked through the park by the beach and let my attention drift between the rhythmic waves and the feel of a smallish guitar in my hands.

Eventually my attention was called elsewhere and I spent my day doing this and that until late in the afternoon when I found myself back in the park by the sea.

A friend of mine—a dynamic French Canadian with a deep accent—was sitting on a bright yellow bench. I sat beside him and listened as he told me of his unexpected plans to return to Montreal. He lamented that he'd brought two lovely guitars with him, but felt he could only return with one and he wondered if he could find someone to buy his parlor-style guitar. He said he would give it away for a hundred dollars but he needed to find someone who would appreciate its beauty and be satisfied with its smaller size.

Manifestation.

I don't know if it was because my recently lost husband was standing in the wings waiting to fulfill my every wish, or because I had pressed in so hard to access the secrets of the universe, or because I spent hours meditating every day, or because the Blue People were working hard on my behalf. But there it was—less than twelve hours from the inception of the desire to its fulfillment.

Manifestation on steroids.

And that was just the beginning.

It seemed nearly everything I thought of, everything I desired, I received in less than twenty four hours.

I longed to see a particular friend. Two hours later she knocked on the door. I missed someone from home. An hour later they called.

And that guitar? Well I really enjoyed it for a while, but I still missed my keyboard. Playing on an instrument you are unfamiliar with doesn't give you the same release as playing on one you can just throw yourself into. I laid in bed thinking, *Maybe I could just have a little keyboard, a cheap one. And MAYBE I wouldn't even have to buy it. Maybe someone was going out of town and wouldn't mind letting me borrow theirs.*

Bingo!

The next morning, I saw my neighbor in the street and she said (I did NOT bring it up, mind you), "Hey, Laura! I know how much you must miss your keyboard and my neighbor is out of town and will not be back until next high-season. I am looking after her stuff and she has a little keyboard she never uses. I am SURE she would be happy to let you borrow it, if you're interested."

I kid you not.

And then there was the school. It was a little English school. The kind that teaches English as a second language to Mexican children. I was following it on-line and decided to see if I could volunteer there when I went back to Mexico, (after I left Mexico thinking I was never coming back).

When I got back in town, I met the teacher in her home. We talked for a half-hour. Then she offered me the school. The entire school! She was looking for a replacement and, after meeting me, she felt I was it.

Occasionally that manifesting thing got out of control.

I didn't take on the school. I had no idea how long I was going to be in town. But, I was so flattered by her offer. And so shocked by whomever was in the wings and on my side. They sure were doing a bang up job!

And then there was the dog.

One thing I learned is that manifesting works when you think about something. You don't necessarily have to think POSITIVELY about it. You just have to feel it on some deeper level. (More about that in NOTES ON MANIFESTING) Well the little town I was staying in was full of women. Older single women. There were so many women, they nicknamed it Puerto Mujeres (Port of Women) instead of Puerto Morelos. Now most of these women swore off men and replaced them with street dogs. I know that sounds awful, but it's true. And I think they didn't really swore off men. I think they just couldn't land one, so they filled the empty space with a dog—or many dogs—and told themselves that they really preferred dogs to men.

Well, I had just been bereft of the most amazing marriage and I had no intention of becoming one of those dog-using, men-lacking women. I was so adamant about it that it was only a short time before a dog showed up on my door step.

You see, I think the Universe doesn't hear the *I don't want* part. I don't think it understands positive and negative. It just hears *dog, dog, dog, dog, dog* because that is how often the thought ran through my head. So it obliged and provide me with a dog.

I wouldn't let her in.

It was four days before I would feed her, but she still followed me everywhere. I walked down the street and she followed me. I went into a grocery store and the owner said, "You can't bring your dog in here!"

I responded with, "She's not my dog."

I sat down at open-air restaurants and she hid under my chair. Friends would comment, "Oh, your dog is so sweet. What's her name?"

And I would respond, "She's not my dog."

For about three weeks her name was She's Not My Dog. But after giving in and feeding her and letting her sleep on my bed, a good friend finally said, "I think you need to change her name."

"What should I call her?" I asked.

"She's My Dog."

Just so you know, since I am sure you must be asking the question, her name officially became Babygirl and all my subsequent adventures included her. In fact, I eventually even named my boat after her.

Be careful what you wish for. Or don't wish for. Or something like that!

There was one other something I manifested during this extreme time. It was 6ft tall with blonde hair and blue eyes.

I put a lot of intention into this one. I got out a piece of paper and made a list. On that list I wrote down the twenty things I most wanted in a soul mate. I missed my husband desperately and believed in love and didn't want to be alone. So, I started thinking of the kind of life I wanted to live. One full of travel and adventure and one close to the sea. Then, from deep within, I pulled up all the characteristics of a man who could walk that journey with me. He needed to be able to handle a boat. He needed to have a big heart. He needed to be from the same place I was from so we would connect easily on cultural issues. He needed to think fast on his feet and be able to fix anything with a roll of duct tape. He needed to be tall because I love tall men, all the men in my family were tall and I felt safe around them.

I wrote twenty things on the list and I gave it to God, the Author of the Universe.

Four days later, I met Lee.

I met him in a dive in Mexico. The most unexpected place to meet the man of your dreams. It was a tiny ex-pat hangout. It was Jimmy Buffet's Margaritaville. It was a place for lost souls to find each other.

I saw him standing over in the corner chatting with people. His name was Lee. He caught my eye. I caught his. The rest is history.

How many things on the list did he fulfill?

All of them.

Manifestation is a powerful thing.

7. NOTES ON MANIFESTING

They say to be careful what you wish for because you just might get it. I appear to be living proof of that.

It seems whatever I think I want, I get. Whatever I put my mind to comes to me, usually in a fairly short time. The weird thing is, often what I think I want, I find out I don't really want after I get it.

Was that confusing?

Example: (I know you already heard some of this, but bear with me.) I left the US for Mexico thinking I wanted to teach English as a second language. I found a little school on-line and talked to the girl who ran it and told her I wanted to do some volunteer work. She was excited.

When I got to the little town where she lived. I was invited over to see the school—which was in her house—and talk about volunteering.

She was super welcoming and I sat on a stool while she puttered in the kitchen and we talked for about a half-hour about our lives and basically just got to know each other. At the end of that half-hour, she offered me the entire school. She said she had been looking for someone to take over and she felt I had been sent to her for just that purpose.

Now what you don't know about me is that I homeschooled my children all the way through high-school and I taught music and art for many years. I LOVE to teach. The idea of having my very own little school was fascinating. But the more I thought about it, the more I felt like it just wasn't the right thing for me. I had just scattered my husband's ashes in the sea and I didn't know if I was coming or going. I didn't know how long I wanted to stay in Mexico. A week, a month, but surely not a life-time. I realized when I was offered the very thing that I THOUGHT would be my heart's desire, I actually did not want it at all.

If it had been several years earlier, I would have fallen off my stool for it. There was something very powerful in my gut, in that place somewhere between my chest and my stomach, that felt how wonderful it would feel to have my very own little school. It was something I had wanted since I was eight and was teaching my next door neighbor how to read. It was a deep seated desire and when I voiced it, even in the mild fashion of wanting to simply volunteer in a little school for a limited time, the universe did not listen to just the words that came out of my mouth. It listened to the powerful feeling behind them.

But when what had once been my heart's desire came to me and I had the opportunity to really examine it in a logical fashion, I realized it came from a past me. Yes, a deep part of me, but a part of me that did not serve my current situation.

So here is my take on manifesting.

It works with emotion. Yes, it works with words and with thinking. But for it to really work like the dickens, there needs to be emotion tied to it.

Let me 'splain.

In the beginning God said, "Let there be light."

God said. He spoke. He thought of an idea. He saw it before it happened. He felt what it would feel like to have light. And He spoke.

When we speak we create vibrations. Everything is vibration. Matter is in constant flux, always moving, always vibrating. So when we speak, the vibrations we create affect our surroundings. That is true. But there seems to be a piece missing or we would all just go around speaking to the mountains to move and having them move just like Jesus told us to. I know so many people who try and try and try to do this but don't seem to get very good results. So what is missing?

Jesus said, "If you believe."

Faith. But it isn't just the kind of faith like, Jesus said it so I believe it kind of faith. Like I am trying to believe in something that is supernatural and I can't see. It is more like gravity. If I drop something, I KNOW it is going to fall. It is a scientific fact. Well so is speaking and changing things. You can explain it with physics. So we need to KNOW that when we speak things are going to change.

There are lots of scientific experiments that have been done that prove this point. One of my favorites was a Japanese guy who spoke to water and then took photos of the crystals it formed. Go look up Masaru Emoto Water Crystal Experiments and look at the pictures. This guy said nice things to some water and awful things to other water and the results were amazing. Also look up Music Sand Patterns and you will find tons of examples of people playing music and creating beautiful patterns in the sand. It's the waves, the vibrations from the music, that jiggle the sand around until it forms itself into complex geometric patterns.

Ok, so if we know, if we can see it with our own two eyes, if it can be proven that our speech changes things, why do we continue to say negative things? If it can be proven that worrying about something and saying negative things about it can bring negative results, why on earth do we do it?

I am as guilty as you are.

I think it's because we run more on feelings than on logic.

Now remember, I am talking about things I have observed, I am not trying to be a scientist.

Think about how you feel when you are in a stadium and people are screaming for their favorite team. Think about how you feel when your favorite song is playing and you turn it up really loud. Think about how you feel when you stand at the foot of a rock-faced, steep-cliffed, mountain and look up, or stand on the beach with the sand between your toes and look out at the moon reflecting off the ocean. Emotions are powerful stuff.

The things we fear come to us. If I am afraid of being alone, terrified of it, I can feel the heart wrenching-ness of it, loneliness will find me.

The opposite of fear is love.

But I am getting ahead of myself.

When we hold powerful emotions deep within us, it colors what we say and how we say it. If we are angry about the world, then everything that comes out of us is colored with hate or despair. Picture the words you say coming out of your mouth having just been in your heart. They are vibrating with the energy inside you, the things that drive you. And when they are released, they are propelled exploding out of a ball of energy in the pit of your stomach like a vibrating ball of colored light, either buzzing and ringing with the shimmering strings of love or pulsing and oozing with the dark dread of fear. You speak and that energy is driven into the grid of the universe that surrounds you and it smashes into lines of power that run into other lines and it colors the strands of space and matter that are attached to you.

Whew....

Feel what is inside you. Picture your fingers with vibrating electricity coming from them, electricity that is colored by what is inside you. What does it look like? Does it knock you off your feet with passion and joy and love for the beauty of the universe or does it leave you breathless and empty with the deep feeling of loss and despair?

We manifest what is inside us.

The energy in us is so powerful that it is impossible for it not to go out into the matrix around us and not color it, thereby coloring our world, our experience, our reality.

So if we want to change what we are manifesting, we need to change how we feel. We need to heal. Our feelings reflect what is really inside us. In fact, they always COLOR our perception. They tell a tale of who we are on the inside. They reveal to us our motivations. Our authentic desires. And it is our desire that creates our reality.

I may say that I want world peace, but really I am angry at the way the government is abusing people and I am filled with hate. So when I speak about world peace, what I BELIEVE inside me at a core level comes rushing out of my gut and colors the words that come out of my mouth. And it isn't peace that is inside of me. I am angry at all the people that do not promote peace. I want to wipe them all aside and create what I perceive to be the perfect world. So what is really attached to my words of peace, is war.

I open my mouth and my beliefs, the ones that are on an almost subconscious level, create my reality and I find myself in a world of constant turmoil. And so I do not manifest what I THINK I want, but I DO manifest what I believe.

And if I can carefully look at what I believe, I may find that it comes from a place of pain.

Getting to the bottom of the authenticity of who we are is not easy. It takes looking at ourselves honestly and without defense. The only way we can truly heal is by looking at what we are really feeling and why. Defending our emotions does not help us. It hurts us. It blocks us. It prevents us from moving forward, from getting unstuck. Because those deep feelings, the real ones, are there for a reason. And if we cannot be vulnerable enough with ourselves to acknowledge them and let them surface so we can look at them clearly, we will never be able to reason with them and heal them.

Not everything in us is negative. We are all a mix. But the over-riding emotions are the ones that rule us.

Back to that love thing.

Love is when we see the hurt, the pain, the suffering. We do not deny it. We feel it. We let it run through us and in it we see beauty. We see comfort, we see compassion, we see appreciation. We rise above the pain and we see the beauty in the world because without the contrast of the dark, the light is never so beautiful. We lift our hands and our hearts and we dance in the rain. We celebrate our breath and the sun and the heat and the coolness and the rain. We smile at a homeless man and he smiles back at us. We play in the dirt with a child who has only an empty soda can for a toy and we laugh as he shows us how the game goes. We get up in the middle of the night when we can't sleep and we look at the vastness of the stars and we know somewhere deep inside us that all of this human experience is designed to teach us to love. It is designed to show us the contrast, the depth of despair and the height of joy and the sameness of our humanness no matter our language or our culture. And we open our arms wide and we feel....and then we begin to manifest joy. It comes to us like a wave of warmth and tingling vibration and it permeates us down to our toes and we are so filled we can hardly contain it and what comes back out of us resonates with this magnificent feeling and our world changes...-

Let go of your fear. Don't let it control you. Allow yourself to feel. Open the floodgates of your emotions. Let them pour out of you. Lift up your eyes. Let the rain come and cleanse you. You WILL manifest what is inside of you, so let it be love.

8. CAVE DIVING

Did I mention I am afraid of the water? Especially dark water?

And most especially dark water that has no known end to it?

You know, the kind that has never been explored and is rumored to be the entrance to the underworld.

That kind of water does exist, and I did go scuba diving in it, and believe me, getting in wasn't easy.

We drove a mile or so down a dirt track through Mexico's Yucatan jungle in a jeep until we reached the entrance to a cave system called Dos Ojos. Dos Ojos means *two eyes* and the cave entrance carries the name for the two separate openings to the fathomless labyrinth below.

The Yucatan peninsula harbors at least 6000 caves, including the longest underground river in the world. Only half of the caves have been explored and many people have lost their lives in the confusing waters deep underground.

My good friend and our dive leader, William, is full blooded Mayan and has done archeological diving in the caves across the peninsula. He said we would not really be cave diving, but only cavern diving. The difference being the ability to always see the light where you came from so, in case of emergency, you can backtrack and find your way out again.

That's what he said anyway…

We carried our dive gear down steps caved into stone and sat at the edge of water so clear you can't even tell it's there. William had very bright, big flashlights for all six in our little party and I clung to mine as I slipped into the cool water.

The cave opening wasn't very pretty. Most of the stalactite tips had been broken off and the rock was dull and grey. The water wasn't very deep, probably only twenty-five feet. I adjusted my weights and sunk to the bottom, testing my buoyancy, which would become very important in the journey ahead.

Then I followed close behind William—and I mean RIGHT behind William—into the cave.

The world transformed.

I felt like I was flying. There is no current in the underground river and the visibility is over two hundred feet, making the water literally as clear as the air. We turned on our lights and an ancient and all natural cathedral of shining limestone stalactites and stalagmites immediately stripped away all my fear. I have never seen anything so beautiful.

As we descended into the cave, the light behind us grew dimmer and dimmer until I could no longer see it at all. Water filled the cave completely. If I ran into any problems, there would be no way to surface. William carried an extra air-tank on his back and in several places along our route more emergency tanks were secured. We followed a thin line that ran the entire length of our dive just in case someone inadvertently stirred up the silt below and our vision became completely obscured.

At the half way point, there was a Y in our path and a sign with a skull and cross bones that warned divers from taking the wrong path.

A flicker of the seriousness of what I was doing brushed my thoughts like a butterfly and only slightly disturbed the yoga-like trance that had come over me with the sound of my rhythmic breathing into my regulator and the pulsing flow of bubbles that floated toward the surface—my escaping breath.

The cave closed in on us.

The jagged stalagmites on the floor below rose up and I rose with them until I realized the ceiling was descending, the two becoming like the ancient jaws of a long forgotten sea monster. I steadied myself becoming aware of my buoyancy in an intense fashion, understanding that a scrape against a pointed giant stalactite tooth might dislodge my air hose from its life-giving tank.

Space closed in until I had maybe six feet of room in which to move forward, carefully keeping William in view at all times.

Then the cave opened up again and a pocket of air appeared above us. We surfaced and, in the damp room, William instructed us to all shut off our lights.

Have you ever woken up in a strange room on a starless night somewhere out in the countryside where not a streetlight could be found? Have you lost your sense of direction and even wondered if you were awake or asleep or maybe dead? Have you struggled out of bed to find the light switch and patted down the walls more and more frantically, trying to maintain your composure and not panic at its inconceivable loss?

Then you know how it felt there in the dark, in the damp, in the Mayan underground.

A flick of a switch and the return of the light brought on an intense feeling of returning to life again. Cave diving? Cavern diving? I think we crossed a boundary that may not have just been a boundary of definitions but rather a boundary of eternity.

Flashlight firmly in hand and very much lit, I sank beneath the water again and back into a world of weightless calm. Soon, disappointment had its bitter way with me as we came into view of sunlight again and the end of our journey.

Given the chance, I will dive the cenotes again—especially under the safe guidance of my scuba-shaman friend. After all, there are many more other-world portals to be discovered.

9. PURPLE LIGHTS

Far out on the Mexico's Yucatan peninsula where the blue-morpho butterflies flit about like the spirits of ancient warriors and the aluxes hide in the jungle waiting to play trick or treat with unsuspecting travelers, there is a rustic hotel. It lies just across the street from Ik Kil, the rainbow-wearing grand cenote that is rumored to be the center of spiritual power for the ruined Mayan city of Chichen Itza.

The hotel has two swimming pools. One pool is manmade. The other isn't.

The manmade pool is round with a pretty fountain in the center. The other pool is a spring. It is an old reef pool with interesting coral formations and tiny caves, small enough for an alux (al-oosh) to hide in. The hotel owner had a pretty, blue-tile border built around it, so when you enter its cool waters you feel like you are entering a swimming pool. But you are not.

You are entering sacred waters.

There is a small, almost un-noticeable sign on the wall in the lobby that explains the limestone pool. It says:

This pool is sacred. Its waters are the power center for the cenote Ik Kil and the spiritual city of Chichen Itza. When you bathe in its waters, if there is anything wrong with you, either physical or spiritual, you will be healed.

I swam in the pool. Of course nothing could keep me from it. I didn't feel anything except a little frightened. The unevenness of its tiny coral caverns made me nervous. I wasn't sure what it might be linked to. The Yucatan is riddled with hundreds of miles of underground caves that are filled with water and I felt sure there must be a link I could not see. My niggling fear that it might suck me under left me a little uncomfortable.

But nothing happened.

Well, nothing happened while I was swimming.

But later that night, something did happen.

The day had been filled with exploring Mayan ruins. After my quick dip in the pool, a traditional dinner of rice and beans in the hotel's restaurant, and a hot shower, I fell into bed. But sleep eluded me.

Pictures flashed in my head so rapidly I could not keep up. Kind of like a commercial on TV where they flash a hundred things a second. One other time in my life I had a similar experience and that was at a lodge in North Carolina where angels are reputed to live. For a hundred years the people who have owned that lodge (and their descendants) have been praying 24/7 and the place is an open portal to heaven. I know. I was there.

But this story is about a little hotel in Mexico.

When I finally fell asleep, I slept fitfully. I tossed and turned, the flickering pictures still flashing through my dreams. And when I awoke in the middle of the night, there were purple lights on the ceiling. I shut my eyes and opened them again. Over and over I checked to see if I was seeing things. Purple balls of light—small ones, about the size of a basketball—floated about six inches from the ceiling. They hovered just at the edge of my vision. If I turned to look directly at them, they disappeared. But when I relaxed and just stared off into space, they floated there in my peripheral vision. I watched them for a half-hour, maybe more, until I simply could not hold my eyes open any longer and I fell asleep.

What were the purple balls of light?

I don't know. I wish I did. I have seen balls of light before. I saw them in that place in North Carolina and I saw them at my house once too. There are people who have insisted they know what the round purple lights are, but I don't think they are correct. How can anyone know for sure? How can people they say they are energy or angels or the spirits of those that have passed unless they have some sort of evidence?

It is easy to think you have all the answers. I am not an all-the-answers kind of person. There are core things that I believe, but I am always learning. And for now, I still wonder what those lovely purple lights were. One day, I hope to know. One day, I am sure I WILL know, but maybe not until I get to the other side of this matrix we all live in.

10. IK KIL

Cenote Ik Kil is considered the power center of the ancient Mayan City of Chichen Itza.

It rests just outside the city and is easily accessible from the narrow Mexican road, after 4-hours of driving out across the Yucatan Peninsula, that is.

The Yucatan has no above ground rivers, just hundreds of miles of rivers that run through an elaborate cave system including limestone stalactites and stalagmites. Occasionally, the ground above the river gives way and a sink-hole is created that provides access into the watery cavern below. These sink-holes are called cenotes. The Mayans believe they are entrances to the underworld, a sacred place they call Xibalba (shi-bal-ba).

The grand cenote at Chichen Itza is intensely beautiful. It drops two-stories underground and is ringed by ceiba trees. Ceibas are the sacred trees that the Mayans believe are home to the goddess of death. Within the damp stone walls of Ik Kil, the vine-like roots from the ceibas hang all the way down to the still pool below, like Tarzan's jungle ropes, but not naked. Rather they are dressed in ferns and brilliant bromeliads. A slender waterfall drops into the cavern and creates a constant mist rife with rainbows fluttering about as the sun's long fingers splay out across the rock.

A carved staircase winds its way around and around until it reaches the level of the pool. It brings casual swimmers and spiritual seekers alike to the edge of the sacred waters.

I fell somewhere between the two.

The day was warm and sunny. We'd driven the old road through small Mexican villages for hours stopping occasionally to water ourselves and connect with the locals. Eventually, we left the villages behind for the long stretch of scrub jungle, a destitute area that leaves you feeling like someone is watching you from between the low palms and strangler figs.

We almost missed the entrance to Ik Kil, it is so unassuming. A small sign marks it—a simple thing on a post that looks as if it was placed there as an afterthought.

A few minutes later we were walking down into the mist.

Did I mention that I don't like dark water?

There is something haunting about the still waters of Ik Kil. Though they are as clear as air, the four-hundred-foot-deep cavern they fall into is as dark as a cloud-covered midnight with no moon and no stars.

And then there is the cave system.

Twenty-feet or so below the surface lie the two entrances to the underground river, one on each side of the cenote. Many miles have been explored via scuba and golden threads strung in the manner of Hansel and Gretel's bread crumbs, but many more have never seen the likes of man.

I held the hand-rail that is nailed into the rock on the way down into the cenote. The mist from the waterfall left the stairs slippery. When I reached the bottom, I just stood for a minute looking up into the colored light. The vines and roots made my think I was in some middle-earth or alux-haunted land.

To my right, rose another stairway. This one ascended to several dive platforms of increasing heights, the highest of which was a good thirty feet above the water. I was not alone. My blonde-haired, blue-eyed manifestation, Lee, was by my side and several pilgrims were already swimming in the dark water.

I did mention that I don't like dark water, didn't I?

When I was three, I moved to Australia. I lived there with my family for five years, and during that time I lived on the shore of a breeding bay for sharks. The water was dark and still, like a calm lake, even though it was surely the ocean. My mother forbade me to go into the water past my knees—which were quite low at the time—in fear of shark attack. One time, a friend came to visit and her mom let her go in swimming. I warned her not to. But she wouldn't listen. (She did not get eaten by a shark. I am just letting you know this ahead of time so you don't worry.) Within minutes of her getting about chest deep in the still sea, a long fin rose out of the water right next to her. She did that running like you are in molasses thing that you do in bad dreams where you can't get away from the bad guy, and I stood helpless, on the shore, watching. I vowed from that time on never to get in still dark water if I could possibly help it.

Knowing there were no sharks in the fresh water cenote did not help one bit. There were grand entrances to a largely unexplored other-world cave system below me.

I really hate it when fear keeps me from doing something, especially something as cool as swimming in the portal to heaven, or hell, whichever the case may be.

So, I climbed the dive-platform stairs all the way to the top and stood looking down, knowing someone else climbed up behind me and was waiting for me to jump. I felt the pressure of them standing at my back, but for a moment I was frozen in my spot. I consciously knew standing there longer would only increase the fear, so I needed to just make a quick decision and jump.

I took stock of the distance to the water below me and the distance I felt I needed to jump out away from the wall to be safe from hitting the rock, and I jumped.

I pointed my toes and held my hands straight above my head to minimize any discomfort upon impact and I hit the water and went down into the dark.

Alone in the deep, I felt the momentum of my body slow almost to a stop, and with a great swash of my arms I pulled myself back toward the surface. When the upward momentum stopped, I was still fathoms deep. So I reached in the direction I assumed was up and gave another great stroke. Still nothing.

This is the moment when you do not panic because you know panicking will only get you in trouble. I wear contact lenses, so I could not open my eyes to see if I could even see the light yet. My breath was still sure in my lungs. I was not drowning. So, I gave another strong swoop and I broke the surface. Moving with great caution, slowly so as not to let on to anyone the great fear I was battling, I wiped the water from my eyes so I could open them and see. Other swimmers were close by and seemed to be having fun, splashing in the cool water. I swam with a controlled stroke over to the make-shift ladder and climbed out as fast as I could.

Swim in a portal to another dimension, check. I didn't even know it should be on my bucket list. It is one of the most amazing things I have ever done.

11. BLACK BETTY

She was a car.

Every car has a life of its own, but this one was exceptional.

Black Betty lived in Mexico, in the Riviera Maya. I don't know where her humble beginnings started, but her late life was spent with me rambling down dirt roads and roads with holes the size of small Mayan pyramids.

She was a Vocho (pronounced bocho), a VW bug turned convertible with a make-shift pleather (plastic leather) top folded down and ready to go up and snap on the moment it rained. Lee and I never actually snapped it on because the snaps were too rusty and, if you drove really fast in the rain, the water shot over the windshield and you didn't get wet anyway.

We found Black Betty sitting outside a small catholic church in the town square in Puerto Morelos, Quintana Roo, Mexico, just south of Cancun. She was sad, neglected, and needed a new home.

So we brought her home.

And we loved her.

One day we decided to buy five loaves of bread and turn them into yummy, toasted ham and cheese sandwiches. We wrapped them in little tinfoil packages, packed them in a cooler, and packed the cooler and our dog, Babygirl, into the squishy backseat of Black Betty. We packed lots of homemade oatmeal cookies in there too.

We crossed town to La Colonia, the traditional Mexican village on the wrong side of the tracks—the local people's town that supported the gringo tourism in the area. Kids rode bicycles down the broken streets. Lines and lines of ticky-tacky houses rubbed shoulders, many wearing clothes-lines parading freshly washed underwear. A grocery store sat on a corner and kids bought little packages of chicken flavor so their mothers could make rice and beans for dinner. A barber shop had young men parading in and out getting fancy swirling designs shaved into their short dark hair. A tiny restaurant boasted white plastic chairs, red plastic tables, and plastic flowered table-cloths. A concrete closet stood on one street corner, the words *Estation Policia* painted in peeling black paint on its side. A young man dressed in an official looking uniform stood outside watching the world go by.

We gave him a ham and cheese sandwich and an oatmeal cookie.

He smiled.

It's a great way to make friends—handing out cookies and melty-hot sandwiches.

We gave them to men digging the foundation of a new house. We gave them to school girls wearing starched white shirts and dark blue skirts and walking hand-in-hand. We gave them to teenage boys ferociously playing games at the video arcade.

Everybody smiled.

They smiled at the cookies and the sandwiches. And they smiled at Black Betty and her chop-top. And they smiled at Babygirl. Every once-in-a-while, I held up Babygirl's paw and helped her wave.

One night, late, when the stars were gone and thunder rumbled overhead, Lee put Babygirl with him in the front seat of Black Betty and drove down a muddy backstreet—deeply muddy and slippery and full of rolling hills. The rain began to pour down from heaven and lightning struck nearby. Lee smashed on the breaks and Black Betty went sliding through the mud and into a tree. Babygirl bolted into the dark. Lee, forgetting Black Betty's wounded condition, bolted after the frightened dog. But Babygirl was nowhere to be found.

Lee came home. Black Betty's passenger-side headlight was cracked and Lee's heart was broken.

Babygirl was gone.

We slept through the night and early the next morning, just as the sun was rising, Lee started Black Betty's engine and returned to the scene of the accident. There was Babygirl, hiding behind a garbage can beside the muddy tracks of Black Betty's slippery slide. She was so excited when she saw Lee, she jumped into our Vocho's very damp front seat and licked him all over. Babygirl was safe. And Black Betty would be fine. She only needed a fresh piece of headlight glass.

When finally, we made plans to leave lovely Mexico for mountains further south, we had to bid Black Betty goodbye. We considered selling her to another owner, but thought better of it and gave her to my daughter who eventually followed me to Mexico. Black Betty had many new adventures, and to this day is still living comfortably in the Riviera Maya where panthers prowl and crocodiles lurk and back roads have potholes the size of small Mayan pyramids.

12. LITTLE AMIGO

We called him Little Amigo. Mostly because he was small, slight, short, petite, slender, wiry. Have I used enough words to describe him? I think not. He was little, yes, even for a Mayan born Mexican. But more than that, despite the language barrier, he was a good friend.

Lee met him on the bad side of town—the part where the tourists never go. Lee was there looking for a part for our VW bug, Black Betty, and Little Amigo had parts stashed in all the corners of his one-room mechanic shop—the one right in front of his one-room house. It was dark and dingy and small like Little Amigo, but it was full of resources often difficult to come by in rural Mexico.

With Black Betty repaired and time on his hands, Lee consented to accompany Little Amigo in a movie fest. They swung together in hammocks in the one-room shack behind the shop and watched old Mexican westerns for hours. They laughed a lot and shared a couple of local cans of beer.

Little Amigo became Lee's go-to man for not just car repair, but other little things that might be needed. He knew everyone in town, so if he couldn't find the right part to fix a water pump or an air conditioner, he knew someone who could. I am still amazed at how well they got along even though most of their communication consisted of hand motions and the phrase "Lets' go, let's go!"

That's what Lee said the day he picked Little Amigo up to go out to the local strip club.

OK, it wasn't exactly a strip club.

Lee showed up at the one-room shack and found Little Amigo dressed in his finest white button-up Mexican-style shirt complete with bow tie, blue jeans, black cowboy boots, and sombrero. Black Betty's top was down and Little Amigo shouted "Let's go, let's go!" as Lee started up the engine and the two skirted potholes, bicycles, sleeping dogs, and street vendors in the road until they arrived at Chuckie's.

I was in Chuckie's once. I left wet—my clothing covered in the beer that I wasn't quick enough to dodge as it flew through the air.

Lee parked Black Betty and Little Amigo jumped out of the car and ran inside. When Lee ducked his head inside the low-ceilinged Mexican bar, little Amigo was nowhere to be found. Lee looked carefully through the locals sitting at the bar in the dim light—hats and jeans and beer everywhere—but no Little Amigo. So he took a seat at a table figuring the short Mayan had run to the gentlemen's room. But when he turned his attention to the crowded dance floor, there was Little Amigo, tapping his heals, slapping his knees, and twirling a heavy set girl 'round the dance floor.

She worked there on weekends, taking tips to allow the local cowboys to dance with her. Dollar bills were tucked in her waist and a good deal of sweat dampened her too-tight rhinestoned shirt. She shimmied and swayed and Little Amigo swayed and shimmied with her.

Lee laughed to himself. Chuckie's was a Mexican version of a very-tame, non-stripping, paid-dancing joint very much enjoyed by locals doing the bachata or the rhumba or simply tapping their heels and slapping their knees and having a wonderful time!

13. THE END OF THE WORLD

It was December 21st, 2012—the day the world was supposed to end. I was living in Mexico and my three children had come to visit for the Christmas holiday.

We got up early and dressed light, it was going to be hot. I piled everyone in the car and we set off down the coast road towards Tulum.

Tulum is a small town about an hour south of Cancun along Mexico's Caribbean coast in a tourist area known as the Riviera Maya. The town is named after the very famous Mayan ruins of Tulum that sit near there on a cliff overlooking the sea. They are beautiful, with foamy waves crashing against the rocks and black iguanas sunning themselves on the clipped grass between the ruins.

But we were not stopping there on this day.

We got to the stoplight on the coast road just at the edge of town and turned right, away from the sea and into the dense scrub of the peninsula. Very quickly, we were out of town and there was nothing but short trees, jungle vines, and brilliant blue-morpho butterflies along the way.

Eventually, we came to a tiny pueblo with a few dilapidated houses, a small store, and a pottery shop selling brightly colored, hand-painted Mexican sinks and tiles. We stopped to get cold coconuts from a man beside the road and then stopped again and bought mango slices dipped in chili powder and lime.

Then we headed into the jungle again.

Did I mention it was the day the world was supposed to end?

The Mayan calendar is very old—26,000 years old. It is divided into five sections of 5,250 years each. It is an amazing calendar predicting cosmic events with incredible accuracy. So when we found out that the last of the 5,250-year segments was at an end on that very day and the entire 26,000 was over, we were a little curious about what would happen, if anything.

Some say the Mayans were not smart enough to create their own complex and forward-seeing calendar. There is a theory that aliens dropped by, handed them some cool stuff, and took off again. Honestly, there are some pictures carved into the walls and stones in the ruins that seem to support such ideas. I saw them. They depict what appear to be spacecraft. But for me, the verdict is usually out until all the evidence is in.

So I took my children deep into the jungles of the Yucatan to stand on top of the second tallest Mayan pyramid in the Americas on the day the world was supposed to end.

Who knows, maybe we would be picked up by aliens.

The thing is: there is some laughter in this, and then there is that niggling thought in the back of your brain that refuses to rule out anything. I am a very spiritual person and, at first, I thought my spirituality and aliens didn't really go together. Now, I am not so sure. I will not bore you with the whole of my philosophy, but let's just say that there are suggestions in ancient scripts, including the Bible, that a race very different from ours was once here. It even goes so far as to say that we may still have some of those very different being living among us. Who knows, maybe the Mayan's information did come from other beings. If you factor that in as a missing puzzle piece, it does help explain a lot.

I have learned that keeping my mind closed gets me nowhere. Admittedly, we are living in a time of shift and I think much truth is coming to the forefront that we did not have access to before. (Well, very few of us did.)

So, we drove into the jungle until we came to a large lake—lagoon really, cut off from the sea—where crocodiles hid in the rushes waiting to be fed by small girls for ten-cent donations from tourists. We paid the obligatory ten cents and watched a dark-haired youngster feed an eight-foot retile. It was probably not too smart of me to lay down on the dock with my face a few feet from the beast in order to take a seriously close-up photo, but I'm stupid like that.

The lagoon was at the base of a rise in the land that the ruined city of Coba was built on. It was just a short drive up the road to the entrance of the park gates. Yes, it is a protected park now, although only two percent of the ancient city has been reclaimed from the giant sacred ceiba trees and suffocating strangler figs.

We paid a small fee and walked through the crooked, wooden gate and into a different world.

Giant structures loomed on all sides. Stones carved with ancient symbols adorned mammoth structures. The ball-court where they played a deadly game—the winner losing his head—stretched out on our left. The mezzanine with its pillars and missing roof was on our left too. In the tangle of underbrush, smaller stone buildings hid, asking us to come explore them. But we had no time for all these things. It was early in the day and we wanted to climb the tower of Nohoc Mul before it was swarmed with tourists. So, we rented bicycles and chased each other down the flat path through the ancient city and through the stunted palms trees until we rounded the corner and saw the temple.

There she stood, one-hundred-and-seven steps high. Giant steps, not stairs to walk up but rather to scramble. On her top was a simple square edifice where priests used to perform their other-worldly duties. We stashed our bikes in the trees and my two twenty-something-year-old boys raced each other to the top. My daughter and I climbed at a little more human pace. Stopping once (OK twice), to catch our breath along the way.

The view from the top swept across acres of unbroken jungle. We could hear howler monkeys off in the distance and see that sparking lagoon where the crocodile lay.

After catching my breath (and pretending not to need to) and allowing the enormity of the scenery to wash over me, I turned to inspect the details at hand. A small, shallow room topped the temple like a bride and groom on a wedding cake. Before it was the blood stone—the alter—the place where those ball-game winners lost their heads. There was a carved channel in the stone to allow the blood to drain, probably into an ornate cup. You would think it would be a gruesome sight, but it wasn't. I suppose time had eroded more than just the stones.

The boys discovered everything there was to see in about three minutes flat. They then pretended to push each other off the temple and into the receiving spiked plants below. They never grow up, those boys of mine. But other than a little jesting and admiring, nothing significant happened. Yes, we stood on top of the second tallest Mayan pyramid in the world on the day the world was supposed to end. But the world didn't end. And the aliens didn't stop by and pick us up.

I have a hunch they may have been watching, though.

14. THE ALUX

An alux (pronounced al-oosh) is a mythical figure from Mayan culture in the Yucatan Peninsula of Mexico. I read once that they occasionally appear as small animals wearing sneakers or button up shirts. This happens when they are caught shapeshifting from their leprechaun-like form to more secretive forms like Tejones (racoon-like critters with long, ringed tails).

Mayan farmers leave offerings out for these unpredictable changelings in hopes of soliciting help in the growth and maintenance of their crops. They fear, if they neglect to leave offerings, the little beasts, (Shhh, don't let them hear that!), may play not-so-nice tricks on them.

Of course, I am breaking all the rules just by telling this story, because you are NEVER, EVER, EVER supposed to mention the word ...*alux*.

I had moved from my little apartment in Puerto Morelos to a grand penthouse a half-hour south in a boating community called Puerto Aventuras. The penthouse was eighteen-hundred square feet of marble floors and glass walls looking out over the Caribbean's sea-glass blue water. I was enjoying the six-month splurge I'd bought myself immensely, swimming in the lap-pool every day and sitting on the palapa-covered porch gazing out at the Southern Cross at night.

When you see the Southern Cross for the first time
You understand now why you came this way

'Cause the truth you might be runnin' from is so small
But it's as big as the promise, the promise of the comin' day

That was until I started hearing voices.

Someone was calling me by name and waking me up as I slept at night. I would bolt upright, jarred from my sleep.

To matters weirder, my daughter, Sarah, and her Mexican boyfriend, Javier, who were staying with me at the time, were sharing my odd experiences. They both confessed they were hearing voices too.

Javi, who understood Mayan folklore, said it was an alux.

I, of course took his comment in stride.

Until the foot prints appeared.

It was early morning and hot. The sun was streaming in the east windows and illuminating the long hallway to the bedrooms. I was a little irritated because there was a trail of water on the floor all the way down the hall. The wet marble tile would be dangerously slippery. I figured someone had showered or been in the pool and carelessly dripped all over. But, as I started down the hall toward my daughter's room to reprimand her for whatever she or Javi did that left that slippery trail, I stopped.

It wasn't just a trail of water running down the hall. It was a trail of wet footprints. Tiny, child-sized, wet footprints.

No children lived in our house.

I carefully avoided disturbing the trail and went to my daughter's room and roused her and her Mexican boyfriend.

"I told you, you have an Alux." Javi insisted they are very real. I could see the conviction in his eyes.

I was left wondering. There was zero explanation for the tiny footprints in the hall. I do believe in fairies, I do. At least I think I do, and I have proof now that something I do not understand exists.

I wonder what else exists that I have dismissed.

PS: My cave-diving shaman friend, William, is full blooded Mayan. He and his wife, Crescent, own a dive shop in my favorite little Mexican fishing village. I asked them if they knew anything about aluxes. William said, "Of course!" and explained how the fishermen see child-sized foot prints in the dew on the boats in the mornings. I had mentioned nothing about the footprints.

15. PICTURE THIS: PENTHOUSE

You wake up in the morning to the sound of the waves. Your walls are open—your glass-walls that push into pockets and disappear offering open-air living high above the sea. The sun is streaming in and you pull yourself out of your king-sized bed and pad across marble floors and into the kitchen. It seems like a really long way to the kitchen. You grind Mexican coffee grown in the highlands and let it work its lovely smellery while you walk out onto the deck and look down at the pool beneath you—the infinity lap-pool that is surrounded by rocky ocean tide-pools. You decide you will go for a swim after breakfast. Your coffee spurts and sputters and announces that it is ready and you pour it into a giant mug, add a little sugar and cream, and go back out onto the porch to soak in the morning rays.

A large iguana pokes his nose over the wall at you. He is probably looking for a few flowers to munch on. You welcome him to the hibiscus growing in red and yellow waves along the overhang. Frigate birds soar overhead and the sky mirrors the color of the sea.

Breakfast consists of over-easy eggs on top of a pile of rice and cherry tomatoes with a few slices of avocado stashed in for good measure. You finish your coffee, put on your swim suit and your silk wrap and flip-flops, grab your thick navy blue beach towel, and head out to your private elevator. It gently brings you down to earth and you exit and walk through flower-covered walkways to the pool. You throw your things on a wooden lounge chair and dive into the cool water. For a moment you refuse to come up, letting the water wrap its glorious morning arms around you. You hold your breath until your lungs burn, and the you explode back into the sunshine.

After a few laps to get your blood flowing, you stop and rest your arms on the side of the pool. A gentle waterfall cascades beneath them and into a trough that surrounds the pool. You gaze out into the waves and let their rhythmic sound lull you into a meditative reverie.

Life is easy. Nature is beautiful. And the deep sadness inside you seems a little less for it.

16. STUCK IN NOWHERE

We drove south. South down the Yucatan's Caribbean coast to a tiny town called Mahahual. It's a beach town, the last on the peninsula. From there, we turned onto a narrow dirt road with a sign that warned us we were entering an area with few people. We drove for another hour through mangroves and across tiny strips of land with towering grasses encroaching on the road. We drove until we came to the end, where Mexico stops and only scuba divers and fishermen know the lay of the land.

The name of the place was Xcalak

One would think that would be the end of our journey. After all, it was the end of the road.

But that one would be wrong.

We slept that night in a grass-roofed hut and the next morning we rose early and ate a small breakfast of fresh fruit and bread and orange-yolked eggs. Then we had our passports stamped out of Mexico and boarded a small fishing boat. By small, I mean a traditional panga, a narrow boat about twenty-five feet in length with no cover to keep off the Mexican sun.

We threw our bags on the bow and sat side by side, Lee and I, and we trusted our lives to a Mexican fisherman who'd spent his whole life navigating the shallow waters and hidden bays where Mexico and Belize meet.

Our captain was short and dark-skinned and spoke three languages: Spanish, English, and Mayan. He deftly turned the boat out into the choppy morning seas and we banged our way down the coast past uninhabited jungle and over swimming-pool-clear water. A half-hour later, we turned inland up a narrow river that wound through mangroves until it poured into the Bay of Chetumal.

It was the most remote place I have ever been.

We were headed to Ambergris Cay, an island off the coast of Belize. Rather than fly, we opted for the scenic route and that included a 3-hour boat tour...*on a three-hour tour.* You remember the song?

Well the weather didn't start getting rough, thankfully. The day was clear and the water in the bay was as still as glass. Turtles bobbed up to catch a little air and small sharks were visible weaving in and out of the seagrass. I trailed my hand in the water and let the sun warm my face. I felt so alive.

We arrived in San Pedro on the far southern tip of Ambergris Cay without incident and we stamped into Belize where we spent ten days wandering down the beach and sampling local restaurants.

And then we headed home.

Adventure often hits when you least expect it.

An hour-and-a-half into the boat ride back to Mexico, the motor quit.

That's when you pull out your cell phone and find your lovely remoteness has left you with zero signal. The captain tried. His friend that accompanied us on the way back through the destitute bay tried. I tried. Lee tried. We floated. We drifted. There was very little wind, but the current took us past one of the many small deserted islands that dot the sprawling bay.

"No problem," said Lee. "We can swim to shore and spend the night on the island."

"Problem," said the captain. "Sharks."

"OK," said Lee. "We can paddle to land and then get off and spend the night on shore."

"No, nada," said the captain. "Jaguars."

"OK," said Lee. "So, we anchor and sit on the boat until somebody comes."

That might be a very long time.

This is where events that could have become life threatening take a turn thanks to modern technology. Apparently, we'd drifted into a spot with cell phone reception. My phone finally had signal. The captain called a friend and a few hours later we had a ride back to Mexico.

I guess pushing the envelope and courting adventure might someday get me into real trouble. But thankfully this was not that day. Grace held us in her hand and we made it home with a story to share.

17. FISHMAN JOHNSON

We were walking. He was on a bicycle. We were on the island of Ambergris Cay in Belize. It's a touristy island in the Caribbean. We were walking down a sandy road just exploring when we came across him. He didn't wiz by. He was carrying a full-sized cooler on the handlebars of his bicycle and he looked a little tired. He was weaving a bit.

We said, "Hi!"

He said, "Hi," back and stopped, balancing his cooler on his bike.

It's cool how you can stop on a sand road in the middle of nowhere on an island and have such a quick connection with someone you've never met before.

We started talking—about what he did all day, about what was in his cooler. He had two lobsters left. He was selling them on the beach. He'd been walking up and down the beach all day carrying his cooler, which was quite heavy when he began. I told him I didn't want to buy the last two lobsters. Even though my hotel had a little kitchen and I could cook, I was out walking and had no idea when I would be back. Carrying lobsters on my impromptu journey didn't really seem like a good idea.

That was when I asked him if he might be able to bring a lobster to my hotel the following day.

"HELLO!"

OK, you have to hear this in your head. It had three parts to it. The HE was low, the LLO was a full octave higher and many decibels louder and the OO part was back toward middling.

I laughed.

In fact, I couldn't stop laughing.

It was just like what we said in high-school when we were being obnoxious, as if to say, "No duh!" or, "Obviously!" or, "Only an idiot wouldn't know that!" or ...well you get the idea.

The power of one word, sing-songed like a high-schooler, took me back in an instant to a time of careless fun and ignorant thinking that I knew everything there was to know in the world—a time when I had the utter confidence only the uninformed can have.

I belly laughed.

He called himself Fishman Johnson. He was the go-to guy for fresh fish. He brought me lobster the next day. And every day after that for the rest of my time on the island.

I listened to his stories. And every time I asked a question that apparently I should have already known the answer to, I had the opportunity to laugh.

"HE--LLO--OO!"

COSTA RICA

18. TIKI BAR TIME TRAVEL

OK, there are some things that, despite my best attempts at logic and reasoning, I just cannot explain.

When we finished our adventures in Mexico, Lee and I moved to the Pacific coast of Costa Rica, to a little hamlet called Manuel Antonio. It's a beautiful mountain town with steep cliffs and gorgeous beaches. Moving there was the culmination of a dream to live in the rain forest and open a little restaurant and B-n-B.

We rented land that already housed a dilapidated restaurant and some defunct bungalows. After months of cleaning and face-lifting, we finally opened a tiki-bar style eatery with some super cute, luxury-camping bungalows in the garden out back.

People started streaming in.

They came from all over. Australia, South Africa, Israel, India—all over Europe and South America. We were thrilled with the diversity of guests we were able to entertain.

We offered live music—a mix of old rock and Latin calypso. We served home-made burgers topped with things like pineapple and bacon, or mango and blue cheese. And we offered the best chocolate-chip cookies in the country.

People came. And they stayed.

Often folks would book a night or two and stay for a week. Or they would book a week and stay for three. The music and laughter went long into the evenings, occasionally sending me to bed while Lee stayed up to manage things.

This was one of those nights.

We had a little house of our own out back with a bamboo wall separating it from the ruckus of the party. I left Lee with our guests and retired to its friendly arms and to my bed. It was getting late, just past 12am. I was exhausted as my day had started with cutting veggies and prepping the kitchen before 6am. Ten or twelve people were still hanging out and chatting with Lee. I could hear them as I pulled the covers up to my chin, glanced at the clock sitting on the little table next to my bed—it was 12:23am—and drifted off to sleep.

I dreamed. Often the sounds of the night slip into my dreams. Music swirled around in my head and I saw myself dancing. One dream flitted to another and another until finally I woke up feeling a little disoriented and achy.

Lee had not yet come to bed.

The sound of talking had not changed. The music still floated in from the restaurant beyond the wall. I looked at the clock again. It was 3:12am. I was surprised and a little irritated. He usually hustled everyone out and closed up no later than 1am. After all, we did have to do it all over again the next day.

Reluctantly, I climbed out from under the warm covers and dressed again. I ran my fingers through my hair so as not to alarm our still-happy guests, and I made my way back out to the fiesta.

Lee was in the middle of some story and a couple of tourists were laughing. The music was still blaring. Nothing had really changed since I'd left. The same people were sitting up at the bar. The same silent news channel was still doing charades on the flat screen TV.

"Are you getting everyone home soon?" I asked Lee privately when he'd finished his tale.

He seemed a little surprised at my irritation. "It's not that late," he said.

"It's almost 3:30," I informed him. He didn't believe me.

I know he loves company and has a tendency to forget about time, but almost three hours was a little extreme. I tried to hide my disapproval and told him I would go get my cell phone so he could verify the time.

3:25am. He still didn't believe me.

We checked the time on the TV. The same. He asked several people he'd been chatting with. They looked at their respective watches and cell phones. The same. Puzzled looks and confusion began to paint people's faces. It had just been twelve-thirty, just a minute ago. There was no way it could be after three. It just wasn't possible.

Somewhere between twelve and fifteen people lost three hours that night. None of us had any explanation for it. I had slept. I felt like not much time had passed, but I was still struggling with the grogginess of half-sleep. I could not confirm my experience but for the clock that *lied* (spelling correct) by my bed.

Our guests however, were shocked, as was Lee. The music was turned off and voices mumbled quietly. People packed their things and said good-night. Cars drove off and guests walked back through the garden to their bungalows. Lee and I closed up the kitchen.

No explanation was ever offered other than the one no-one wanted to admit. We time-traveled.

19. CHICKEN BONE

There is a little town called Quepos that sits at the bottom of the Manuel Antonio hill on the raging Pacific Ocean. In the little town is a little park with brightly colored benches in peeling paint and towering mangoes trees that look like something out of the garden of Eden.

I occasionally sat on those park benches, waiting for this or that, usually a taxi to take me home, up the hill that only a mountain goat could climb. Often the locals would come and sit with me, or try to sell me something, or beg for a bit of cash.

Only once did someone try to sell me a chicken bone.

A used chicken bone.

A rather tallish man wearing an old t-shirt and dusty blue slacks approached me as I was sitting on my bench. He leaned into my space and, I must admit, he didn't smell very good. But, I am not usually offended. I try to look past smells and such and see what is in front of me. This time, it was a mostly-eaten chicken leg. And in front of me it was, thrust very close to my face.

The tallish man was thin. His matted hair was curly and mostly grey. He spat a little as he spoke. Involuntarily, I leaned back while still trying to appear polite. I listened closely, trying to understand what he was saying as he rambled on, but my Spanish wasn't very good and his speech was a little slurred, probably due to the tequila on his breath.

I did pick up the words *chicken* and *ten cents* and I thought I heard the word *buy*, which seemed a little confusing.

As I sat there wondering how I could get myself a little farther away from the meatless, waving bone without seeming too rude, another local street person came to my rescue.

"He wants to know if you want to buy his chicken bone," he offered.

"He will sell it to you for ten cents."

Ten cents was cheap, but I didn't buy the used poultry. In retrospect, maybe I should have. Can you imagine the price a used chicken bone purchased from a poor man at a seaside park on the Pacific coast of Costa Rica could bring on eBay? I might have made a million.

20. FALLING OUT OF THE SKY

Manuel Antonio, Costa Rica is a group of homes, shops, and eateries nestled in the rain forest on a steep, winding hill that snakes along a cliff overlooking the Pacific. Three different kinds of monkeys swing through the trees, five-foot-long iguanas show off red frocks and green jeweled necklaces in the middle of the road, snakes long enough to stretch across the entire road hide in the rafters of palapa-roofed restaurants, and passionfruit colored scarlet macaws swoop through the branches of the mango trees.

A thousand-dollar-a-night hotel and nature reserve sits high above the winding road. We went there for dinner occasionally, leaving our van in the parking lot and taking the white-kid-gloved golf cart shuttle up the devastatingly long, steep driveway.

I loved the restaurant on top of the hill. It was possible to see all the way to Jaco (ha-ko), a surf town an hour away, and the sunsets out over the deep blue ocean were stunning.

That particular evening was clear and the sun burned the color of a ripe mango, all juicy and dripping into the sea.

A classical Spanish guitar sung the Hawaiian version of Somewhere Over the Rainbow as our blueberry and thyme martinis were served alongside tapas plates filled with gorgonzola cheese tarts, mahi-mahi ceviche, Caribbean honey calamari salad, and sweet plantain pie. As delicious as the food was, the view would not be ignored with its giant hand-shaped rocks that grabbed the surf and flung it all white and foamy toward shore. Below us macaws circled, their piercing cries announcing the end of the day.

That was when we saw the bright light of what looked like an airplane headed straight toward us. Such an odd place for an airplane. There was nothing to land on along the rocky cliffs and the airport in the palm groves behind the hills would require a very different approach. We watched it come closer and decided it must be a helicopter, although that too seemed unlikely given its position.

Then, out of the blue, Lee said, "Just watch, I bet it's going to fall..." and he finished his sentence as it fell, "...out of the sky."

There is nothing below where the bright light fell, just a rocky shore and a very steep cow pasture—no safe place for anything to land.

I sat there with my drink in my hand—forgotten, my mouth slightly ajar, and no breath on my lips.

Fall wasn't really the correct word for the behavior of the bright light because falling isn't really fast and the light rushed into the ground, or more likely the sea.

There was no splash that we could see, neither was there any smoke or evidence of a crash of any sort.

It simply disappeared.

And, this is where theories abound and imagination takes over.

I, personally, decided the most logical explanation was an underwater base in the deep ocean just off the shore of one of the least populated countries on earth.

It certainly seemed plausible.

After all, there must be a conspiracy of alien life and the global illuminati government preparing for the total takeover of mankind somewhere in the wings.

You think I jest.

I am not so sure.

21. JUKE BOX HERO

It is difficult to write this bit without being emotional. I am not sure why, as it does not appear so on the surface. So, I will write and we shall see what becomes of it.

There is a beach along the edge of town in Quepos, Costa Rica. It isn't a nice beach. In fact, you cannot lay in the sun there because, when the tide comes in, it comes with a roar, swelling and rising against the sea wall. At high tide, the fishing boats can motor over the sand bar and into the harbor there, but at low tide they are stranded, some listing sideways, their hulls in the sand.

There is a park—a nice park as far as Central American standards go—along the sea wall. School kids practice drum-lines there in the evenings and two days a week the feria (farmer's market) erects its row of white-roofed fruit and vegetable stands.

I love the feria.

You can buy fresh-pressed sugar-cane syrup, and mangoes in all sizes, and sweetened oatmeal smoothies, and potted basil and rosemary, and yucca roots with the dirt still clinging to them, and red spikey mammon chinos, and grilled meat-on-a-stick, and bananas so sweet and ripe and... well, the list is never ending.

We parked the van and wandered down the boardwalk. I filled bags with produce for the week and we bought chicken and cheese filled empanadas to munch on.

But this story doesn't really start until we climbed back into the van. That was when we saw him. He was sweeping. He was sweeping an empty lot across the street from the feria. Well, it wasn't exactly empty. It was filled with stuff: an overstuffed chair with the stuffing falling out, a pile of discarded tires, empty cardboard boxes, rusted and barely recognizable small appliances, and a crib...a pink baby crib.

And there he was sweeping. Or maybe dancing. I am not quite sure. But he definitely had a broom in his hands and he was swirling around with it.

I climbed in the van, stuffed my bags behind the seat, bit into a lukewarm chicken pastry, and watched him. Lee didn't bother to turn on the van. The show was far too entertaining.

This is where it gets hard to write, and I really don't know why.

He was wearing a thin coat, pulled up on only one arm and hanging down around his bare knees like a one-sided, royal cape. His shorts were striped and loosely tied about his waist, drooping a little more than I would personally have been comfortable with. On his other arm was a radio—the big boom box kind—with one speaker removed. Somehow he stuck his arm through the space and he had it pulled up almost to his shoulder like a lady might wear a handbag. On his head was a basketball hoop. (This is not made up, I swear!) The basketball net was hanging down over his face like a fancy veil. And in his hands was a straw broom with which he was sweeping and dancing.

I think I stopped chewing.

He was lost in a reverie and, afraid I would break it, I found myself becoming as still as a manikin in a nice clothing store. Still, somehow he noticed me, or us. Lee was sitting in the driver's seat, shushing me even though I was silent. He, like I, understood we were watching something spectacular.

The dancing, sweeping man noticed us even though we were half a block away sitting manikin-still behind the glass of a minivan windshield.

That was when he got angry.

He came at us with the broom, now a lethal weapon, a javelin. He ran into the middle of the street and held it high and threatened us like a warrior on a battle field. And then he did the unthinkable.

He threw his dance partner/javelin to the ground, dropped his loosely tied shorts and waved his you-know-what at us as if to say the most insulting, degrading things a modern street warrior could say.

I turned my face away.

Lee started the van and we had no choice but to drive right past him. He grabbed his broom up off the pavement and ran at us, butt end of his weapon aimed at my slightly opened window. Lee swerved and we sped away.

We named him Juke Box Hero.

A little post-show research turned up some interesting information about the hero of the play. He had apparently fried his brain with too many magic mushrooms in his early days and he wasn't really homeless. His family owned the house next to the not-so-empty lot and they let him use the space. At a later date we actually saw him sleeping in the pink crib and several times we saw him relaxing in the overstuffed chair. After his riveting performance, he was definitely on our radar.

In fact, I was sad the day I saw the garbage truck haul his crib away.

And in truth, I cannot blame him for being angry with me. How would I feel knowing someone was watching me from behind closed van doors? I would probably feel as violated as he did.

It is hard to get inside the head of a man whose brain has been fried by mushrooms. But regardless of what was going on in there, he obviously still felt a need for some decency. I watched him from a distance and much more carefully in the days to come, hoping for an opportunity to get into his world, but I never did have much of a conversation with him. Well, there was that bit about the frozen fish, but that is another story.

22. WOULD YOU LIKE A FISH?

Juke Box Hero was in fine form that afternoon. He wore a long, green coat on his lanky body and a feather boa around his neck. It wasn't cold in the streets of Quepos along the Pacific beach. But, it wasn't hot either. It was the rainy season where water falls so hard from the sky you wonder if you fell off a boat and you are flailing in the surf.

It wasn't raining.

In fact, the sun was struggling to break through the low clouds.

But Juke Box was dressed for chill. He was wearing those half gloves with the fingers cut off when he presented me with the fish.

We slowed the van to a stop and rolled down the window to say, "Hi."

It had been at least a week since our first introduction to the tall, homeless man and we wondered how he was doing. He noticed us immediately.

"Would you like a fish?" he asked holding a stiff, icy, thin, black fish in his tipless-gloved fingers.

I smiled, a little taken back, but appreciative of his generosity.

"No, thank you," I answered.

He looked a little disappointed, so I quickly followed it up with, "You can take it home and cook it for dinner."

He paused, considering the logic of the suggestion, nodded his head, smiled appreciatively, turned and walked away.

Sometimes the memories that stick with you the longest were of the shortest events.

This was that.

23. SPINNING THE HAT

Lee has a hat. Well, he used to have it. It has long since unraveled and turned back into a pile a straw. But Lee had a straw hat that he wore all the time, no matter how battered and silly it looked.

There was a reason it was battered.

He spun it like a basketball.

Lee loved to play basketball, and in all our travels he made sure to carry his basketball with him. He played with a lot of kids in the street and he made a lot of kids laugh by demonstrating his amazing ability to spin it balanced on his finger.

But carrying a basketball everywhere you go, like to the grocery store or the little *soda* (local Costa Rican restaurant) was not very practical.

So he bought a straw hat.

And he learned how to spin it.

Well, one day we were walking down a narrow back street in Quepos, just off to nowhere-in-particular, and a skinny, old black man came along walking the other way. Lee was wearing his straw hat. The black man was also wearing a straw hat. In fact, he was wearing the exact same straw hat, probably purchased at the feria just like Lee's.

We said, "Hello!" and Lee pointed to both hats. Language barrier? When you speak charades fluently, there is no such thing.

The old man put his hand to his head, understanding that both he and Lee were wearing the same hat. His reaction was sweet—recognition dawning in his eyes and pleasure quickly spreading across his face.

But when Lee took his hat off his head and spun it on his finger-tip like a wobbly, tattered basketball, the old man slapped his knee and couldn't stop laughing!

24. CANS AND GUILT

He sat on the side of the road, just inches from traffic. He sat huddled beneath a black plastic bag and almost completely hidden from view. A huge pile of crushed cans lay next to him. At first we didn't see him. We saw the cans, piled in the rain, and we wondered why they were left so close to the side of the road.

In Costa Rica, when it rains, the roads become treacherous. Rivers of water run in torrents down the steep winding hillsides, sometimes washing the blacktop away. Visibility is reduced to almost nothing and, on the extremely narrow lanes, accidents are often and deadly.

So a huge pile of crushed cans just inches from the traffic was cause for concern.

We slowed just out of curiosity and then saw him, sitting next to the cans and covered in a black plastic bag. A quick replay of the day's events in my mind brought up the big black bag and a teenage boy picking up cans on my mind's TV screen. He must have gotten caught in the storm and dumped all the cans out of the bag so he could climb inside for some shelter.

We didn't stop. We drove by too quickly in the rain. We could have gone back, but we didn't. I can tell myself that it would have been too dangerous to stop there on the narrow hillside, but that would not have been the truth as the boy was hiding from the rain at the entrance to a restaurant and we easily could have pulled safely into the driveway.

It was cold. I was wrapped in a sweater. I was shivering in my sweater. I let my mind drift to feelings of how cold the boy might have been and how wet he must have been despite his plastic protection.

We could have brought him a hot cup of coffee. Or better yet, we could have put all his cans in the back of our van and brought them to the recycling office instead of leaving the boy to carry them up the hill. I knew how steep that hill was. I walked it in good weather and had to stop three times to catch my breath in order to get to the top. And I walked it empty handed.

Sometimes you stop to help. And sometimes you don't. It doesn't mean you don't want to. In fact, it may tear at your soul for hours or even days afterwards. You see a little bit of someone's story, but you miss the part after you might have stepped in. You don't know where the story line went. You put down the book and lose the thread.

What was his name? Did he have a place to sleep at night? Why was he sitting so close to the road? Was he freezing under that empty trash bag? How old was he? How would his life have changed, or not changed at all, had I stepped in?

My questions would never be answered. And though, since not-stopping, a hundred rain storms have come and gone, my guilt has still not completely washed away.

25. EL SILENCIO

El Silencio is an entity unto itself. A town in the lowlands on Costa Rica's Pacific coast, it has an other-ess, a removed-from-the-world-ness, a something-is-under-the-rug-ness that lingers in its shaded palm groves. Turn off the main highway and follow the dirt road around the bend where the towering wide-rooted ceiba tree stands sentry and cross the river on the narrow, guardrail-less bridge with the sign that warns you not to fall off. Pass the palm-ringed soccer field and the carpenter's shop with the piles of teak out front and you will find yourself passing tiny cement houses painted in bright pinks and blues and greens and apricots and tangerines. Stop there. Pull in at the mini-super—the tiny grocery store on the right, the one with the peeling blue benches out front—and you will find yourself at the spot where the smiling boy rode madly by on his bicycle.

I don't know if he was deaf, but I wondered. He never spoke. But he did smile a lot. The other boys gave him some respect, as if he were the younger brother who needed to be carefully watched and yet allowed to live freely. We bought him an ice cream sandwich which he devoured promptly.

We watched for him every time we drove into town, which was often. It was a safe haven for us. A place removed from the craziness of running a hotel and restaurant in a foreign country. We escaped there, in the quietness. Having made our purchase at the small store, we chose a rutted path off the dirt road and drove our van down into the vast sea of towering red-berry oil-palms.

El Silencio is a town set aside as a co-op owned by the people who lived there. It is nearly completely self-sustaining with a chicken farm, an organic community garden, a furniture-building shop where local teak is turned into beds and chairs and tables, and a thousand acres of very profitable oil-palms. Wagons drawn by brown and white oxen with huge humped backs haul bright red oil berries from the depths of the groves to the buttered-popcorn smelling oil plant out on the main road. Wiry men in high-water pants and thick snake boots use sickle-topped poles to cut the berries from the high branches of the trees. Women and children brave the snake infested, palm-branch-littered ground to gather the berries that fall from the piled-high wagons.

When we needed to escape, we drove so far into the groves that all noise but the squawk of the crows was eaten by the trees. We turned off the engine and rolled down the windows. The earthy scent of rotting greenery drifted in. We sat in silence. Sometimes we fell asleep. Sometimes we braved the snakes and got out of the van to pick through the strewn branches for a few stray berries to bring home.

The day the boy rode madly by, we'd been in the grove for an hour or so and were heading back to the business of our business. We pulled out of the rutted path and back onto the dirt road and stopped across from the mini-super. Lee got out of the van with the intention of buying us each an ice cream sandwich. He stopped for a moment to stoop and pick up something in the road, something that caught his eye, maybe a bright green El Silencio dollar bill. (The community even had its own currency.) I don't remember. In fact, I may never have known what it was he stooped to retrieve. I watched for traffic from the safety of my seat. I don't know how I missed the boy. I don't know how he rode so fast. Suddenly he was there, peddling like the Wicked Witch from Dorothy's Oz and smiling like Alice's Wonderland Cheshire cat. Like a whirlwind, he peddled madly past, leaving Lee and me reeling. We were left there in his dust, feeling the brunt of his frozen smile. For a moment we both remained in shocked silence.

Perhaps that is why they call it, *El Silencio*.

26. THE BAT HOUSE

We called it the bat house. It was the big house on a four-hundred acre Costa Rican ranch that abutted the sea. The house was lovely, but for the spaces in the walls in one bedroom where you could see outside and the tilt of the floor that had me chasing anything I dropped to the other side of the room.

And there were bats.

No mosquitoes—which is a good thing in a country where dengue fever can put you down for a month or more, or possibly even take your life.

I was thankful for the lack of the tiny pestering creatures, but I did not know they were simply a depleted food source for a greater threat.

I thought there were mice in the walls. I could hear scratching and scattering, especially at night. Mice are really cute when they come from the pet store, so I wasn't too afraid, although I didn't relish them crawling through my things.

But, even though a mouse did once run across my pillow while my head was on it, I finally had to come to grips with the fact that the scratching in the walls was not mice.

The evening was late and the moon was waxing. Trees with feathery leaves towered over the farm house, blocking most of the light from the moon.

I stood outside, my neck strained from looking up, trying to see though the forest to gaze at the moon, when that magical hour came and the bats left the roost. Hundreds of them winged from my rafters. A thick line of flying black burst from the roof, and I knew at once I must move. Not just move my feet and run, but move all my things out of the house—the house I had just moved into.

I was disappointed. I loved the bat house with its wrap around porch and its vaulted ceilings. I loved the teak table that was so heavy I could hardly drag it across the floor. I loved the cows that ambled though the yard and the horses that whinnied at night when I was drifting off to sleep.

But I didn't love the bats.

And I didn't love the man that hid under the house, lying in wait to sneak into the kitchen and steal my purse—my purse that was packed with all my credit cards and cash and all my ID, including my passport.

Weeks before I witnessed the bats fling their bodies toward the moon, my psyche was violated. My inner-core was rocked. My illusion of safeness was exposed.

I had stashed my full purse by the door because we were getting ready to leave to do our passport run to Panama early the next morning.

The dogs had been restless all evening, running outside and barking at nothing, or maybe the developing moon, or maybe the bats I didn't yet know were living in the ceiling.

We were packing a few things and looking forward to a road trip across the mountains on the Via de La Muerte—The Way of Death. It is beautiful there.

We walked into the bathroom talking and packing and cleaning. That was when I heard a shuffle on the porch. Possibly, a racoon, but not quite. It was heavier.

We looked at each other with some concern and hurried out into the great room. We stepped out onto the porch and saw nothing but moonlight drifting through the trees.

All seemed well, but for an unsettled feeling.

An hour later, we readied ourselves for bed and I went to find my contact lens case which I left in my purse. That was when I discovered my purse was missing. It had been sitting on the shelf near the door. A quick inspection revealed that nothing else inside was missing. But, several tools had been taken from the small shed on the porch.

Did I mention that the bat house sits in the middle of a field on four-hundred acres of land next to the sea?

Except for the ranch hands in the little house though the woods, there is no one else within screaming distance.

I suddenly felt very vulnerable. I wanted to stay inside and shut off the lights so no one could see where I was or what I was doing. I wanted to let my eyes adjust to the dark so I could spot my intruder if he was still lurking under the eaves. I was afraid of finding him lest he use force to free himself and I find myself boasting a bullet wound. Not something I relished having.

I did not sleep.

I did not sleep for weeks.

We postponed our trip and attempted to find my purse with all its important papers. We went on the banana coconut diet because we had no cash, no ATM card, and no passport to use as ID to pick money up from a Western Union.

We didn't drive much because we had no money for gas. We dragged the mattress out into the living room every night to get away from the mouse that ran over my head.

I loved the bat house.

It is disappointing when you think you have found something wonderful and it turns into a nightmare.

I did not sleep for weeks and finally, after that night with the waxing moon and the swarm of bats leaving their roost in the rafters, we packed our things and left.

27. THE PATH TO THE SEA

Upon our arrival to the bat house, we were thrilled to discover there was an old path through the barrier mangroves that led down to the beach. We wasted no time in hiring the young ranch-hand who lived in the little house through the woods to show us the way.

It was a clear, June day and we decided to bring our two rescue dogs with us. Lee wore sneakers and I opted for flip-flops since the day was hot.

That was mistake number one and mistake number two.

David (pronounced Da-veed) lead us away from the big house and down a machete-ed path through an over grown field where several horses munched on grass and avoided us and our dogs. Tiny yellow wildflowers grew among the weeds and I stopped to see if they smelled good. They didn't.

Charlie and Babygirl ran like wild pups back and forth along the path until we came to a thicker grove of wild hedges and I insisted they stay closer. We rounded a curve and came to a steep drop off with a very brown river not exactly raging, but not exactly trickling either, between us and the opposite shore. David explained there used to be a bridge crossing the river, but it was no problem. He knew another way.

So we turned away from the sound of the sea and headed upstream, staying relatively close to the bank. Soon David was using his machete to clear an old path. We meandered closer to and further away from the water until we came to a clearing along the edge of the water. David looked with some hesitation along the bank.

"Cocodrilos?" I asked (Crocodile. And in Costa Rica, they grow easily to four or five meters. That's twelve to fifteen feet.)

"Only babies," was the not-too-convincing response I received.

Not asking where the mother might be, I tried to shove down that nagging feeling that I was getting more of an adventure than I had asked for. We marched on, away from the water again and this time through very thick brush. It took some time for David to clear us a narrow path and I began asking if we should turn back.

"No problemo."

Soon we were at the water's edge again. This time it was just a shallow, clear pebble-strewn stream—just a little more than ankle deep.

Charlie bounded across the water after David and Lee, but Babygirl refused to get her feet wet. Under the conditions, I can't say I blame her. Remember what I said about mistake number one? I tried to pick her up, but she escaped me and ran along the bank downstream. That left me on one side of the water and Lee on the other with me chasing a dog down a slippery, rocky bank into unknown territory.

I won't make more out of than I should. It was very frustrating and took some time, but no real danger ensued and eventually I got her in my arms and was able to cross to the other side.

And into the mangrove muck.

The tide was out and we had officially entered the mangroves. I thought the whole point of this adventure was to find a path that avoided the tangled roots.

At first it wasn't too bad. I stayed on top of the roots and jumped from tree to tree avoiding most of the muck. But after a while, the trees became less dense and the roots further apart. I found it difficult to leap that far and found myself trying my luck with stepping onto the earth below.

Then there was mistake number two. Flip flops. They come off your feet really easy. And they stick in the molasses quicksand. After trying my luck at venturing from the relative stability of a mangrove root and finding myself knee deep in oozing, oily, black muck—after grabbing a nearby lifeless-arm looking branch and hauling myself back to safety with the help of both Lee and David, I was almost unable to retrieve my shoe. Some strong hand from the Creature of the Black Lagoon had an iron grip on the it.

So the crazy thing is, while I was trying to rescue my shoe—and myself—from the sucking blackness, two young teenagers appeared, clad only in flip-flops and bathing suits. They were fresh and clean and fairly skipped along, like two pixies come out of the woods.

I watched them flit by—wondering where on earth they had come from—until they were gone, apparently down the path to the sea, the path which I could not see for the life of me.

I think that was when I wondered if we would ever make it home again. Hours had gone by, and when and if we finally got to the beach, we still had to walk home.

I did rescue my flip-flop and figured out how to use not just the roots, but the base of the trees, to wend my way carefully along the path that only I was unaware of.

Eventually, we came out of the mangrove swamp and back to the river again. This time it was a raging chocolate milkshake. David was quick to explain that we were almost there. The crashing waves could finally be heard nearby and we only had to get in the middle of the now-much-deeper-wider river and walk in it, dowstream (with the cocodrilos hiding somewhere in its chocolaty depths) to the open ocean.

I cannot believe my stupidity. I actually got into the river. Lee carried a squirming, terrified Babygirl high over his head and David carried Charlie. We walked for only a few minutes. My stupidity meter was pegged and a creepy feeling had its clawing fingers around my neck and was threatening to drown me. I could NOT walk any further. I HAD to get out.

David agreed. In fact, even he seemed nervous, and that could not be a good thing. So when I expressed my need to get out of the water he piped up with a cheery, "No problemo," we could just go back through a little bit more mangrove and then we would be at our destination.

I tried not to appear completely panic stricken as I climbed back on the bank and—thankfully, this time—entered the marsh. It was much firmer. Sand made up most of the ground so close to shore and I could actually walk between the now sparsely growing trees.

We came around another bend and the beautiful, shallow water where the river meets the sea met my sore eyes. It was so clear and wide and shallow. I dashed across the now harmless looking river and found myself standing on a beach that looked like something out of Gilligan's Island. Palm trees grew almost down to the rolling waves. Mountains rose into the mist off in the distance. Pelicans swooped and played, looking for fish. And then there was the 4-wheel drive truck parked in the sand.

4-wheel drive truck?

And what about those teens that flitted along the path I could not seem to find?

And how would we get back home, no matter how remote and beautiful this beach seemed?

No probelmo.

We were standing just feet from a hard-packed sand road that ran along the beach and back out to the main road not a mile from the big house on the four-hundred acre ranch.

Apparently when you ask for the path to the beach, you should be very specific.

It only took about a half-hour to walk home—the dogs running back and forth like young pups and me with my flip-flops in my hand.

28. HEAVEN ON EARTH

We'd been driving for weeks through Costa Rica's rainforests and fields of green. We had taken the seats out of the back of our van, replaced them with a full-sized mattress, packed a travel bag, and left our home in Manuel Antonio for points unknown.

We'd seen rainbow eucalyptus trees and plantations of pineapple and sugar cane. We'd been to beaches where you couldn't see another soul for as far as you could see. We'd even been on the slopes of several volcanos. But what came into view as we drove through the cloud forest in the north central mountains was more stunning than anything I had seen in a very long while.

We drove around a wide bend on the top of the mountain and there, below us, rolled a steep valley covered in coffee bushes shaded by banana trees. Mist fell into the deep ravine and a fine rain rained below us. Nestled at the bottom of the ravine sat a grass-roofed shack and just above it on the mountainside a spindly middle-aged man with a broad-brimmed straw hat swung a machete.

We pulled over and got out on the narrow stretch of road. I felt like I'd stepped into a National Geographic magazine.

The man was so far below us that we could not hear a sound he made. The land was so steep; I don't know how he found a foothold to tend to the bushes. I walked to the edge to peer down and get a better view and noticed that I didn't have to look far to see the bright red coffee beans. The round bushes grew all the way up the hillside to the edge of the road I was standing on. I picked a few of the shiny berries and put them in my pocket for a keepsake I knew would probably perish before I even got home. But, I couldn't help myself. I love coffee.

I have roasted my own green beans in an old-fashioned popcorn popper—the kind you hold with a really long handle over an open fire. The smell of the roasting beans is rich and fragrant and when the heat gets high enough, the skins pop open. It sounds just like popcorn. You shake the pan until the popping stops and then open the pan and pour the popped beans into a big shallow bowl and take it outside into the wind. Then you swirl the bowl allowing the paper-thin skins to come to the surface and be blown away leaving only the dark-roasted coffee ready to be ground into something heaven sent.

Now, here I was looking down into a valley of coffee, in the rain, in the high mountains of one of my favorite coffee countries, Costa Rica.

I had a good friend who opened a little coffee shop near my home in The States. He traveled to countries in Central America where he purchased fair-trade coffee beans directly from the farmers. I was fortunate enough to be in on a coffee tasting he hosted when he first opened his shop and was mixing up his own special blend.

Little white cups of strong, black Joe lined the counter at the tasting. Each had simply a number before it and the idea was to rate each sample without knowing anything about its origin. After sampling probably twenty different cups, I chose my favorite. When the number were turned over I discovered I loved a Cost Rican coffee from the little town of Tirrazu.

Which brings me back to the mountainside and to my hungry belly.

Reluctantly, after soaking in as much of the view as humanly possible and taking pictures that could in no way do the scene justice, we climbed back in the car and made our way to a little lower elevation and a small town in search of a bite to eat. It was late afternoon and, though we were looking for a typical Costa Rican restaurant, the only thing we could find was Italian. It seemed a little odd in the rain forest and all, but we were thankful for a dry place to sit inside and get something to eat.

I ordered a plate of homemade pasta with ruby-red tomato sauce and a cup of local coffee. The waitress brought out a wooden stand with a linen bag hanging from it. She carefully poured ground coffee into the bag, put a small white mug underneath it, and poured hot water though the rich smelling beans. I watched and waited, enjoying the authenticity of the moment. When the cup was full, I pulled it from under the linen bag, added a little hot milk and raw, local sugar and sipped.

Oh, My!

What Joy!

I sipped again and savored the nutty, roasted flavor of the fresh beans.

I scarfed down the homemade ravioli and had a second cup of coffee, relaxing into a warm and satisfied feeling that seemed to envelope me.

When we rose from our little red-and-white-check covered table, I had to ask if I could buy a bag of the coffee I just savored.

You know where I am going with this by now, don't you?

It was Tirrazu coffee, and I had some of the fresh beans still in my pocket!

I think maybe we get to request a copy of a little bit of earth when we get to Heaven. If that is true, the coffee plantation on the steep slopes of Tirrazu will be my pick!

29. THE MOTHER EARTH TREE

We saw her standing on the roadside along the winding way to the top of the volcano. She was beautiful and tall and her limbs hung down, covered with orchids and ferns and bromeliads. Around her feet were toadstools, a whole forest of them, offering shelter to small creatures needing to escape the rain.

She was old. How old, only the wind knows. Her bark was wrinkled like the skin of an old Native woman who'd spent a hundred years in the sun. Her girth was so vast that a hug would only wrap around a small portion of her immensity.

I touched her trunk—held my hand there for a moment, just feeling whatever I might feel. Aside from roughness and dampness and softness, I felt a settling come over me, a calmness that drove away my angst as if by magic and made me forget that such things existed.

The old volcano spared her during its last eruption. Its molten rock and hot ash was flung down another slope, away from her spacious spot. I do not think she could have uprooted herself to escape, so I am thankful her life was spared.

So she still stands, flowers and fiddleheads in her hands. And I am grateful for the brief connection we made—she and I—on the side of the road on the way to the top of the volcano.

30. ERUPTING VOLCANO

We'd been on vacation on Costa Rica's Caribbean coast and were driving home through the vast stretches of banana plantations that cover the lowlands and sweep to the sea. Small villages came and went and dark-skinned kids on bicycles scooted out of the way of our minivan.

After an hour, the short banana trees gave way to taller mango and towering breadfruit trees. The hills began to rise.

Costa Rica is divided in two by the Talamanca mountain range. The spine of the country, it rises into the clouds. Steep cliffs and deep ravines offer breathtaking views along the winding road that is, in part, known as Via de La Muerte, or the Way of Death. The climb pops your ears and has you clinging to your seat as you pass what I like to call *instantaneous death drops* where the land falls away and you cannot see the bottom of what could be a very long plummet.

We headed toward the cloud forest, passing coffee plantations that were shade grown under finger-paint eucalyptus trees. We wound around rolling fields of spikey low-growing pineapple and waving fields of sugar cane. Occasional hat-topped, machete-bearing farmers guided produce-filled, cart-bearing oxen down the road. We stopped and let them pass and admired the easy simple life painted on the scene before us.

Eventually, we left the fields behind. The air grew chilly and a primary forest of fern and bromeliad laden trees lined the narrow curving road.

When we began our journey, the Caribbean skies were sunny, but as we neared the mountain spine, the weather began to change.

It rains often in the mountains. Torrential, you-can't-see-your-hand-in-front-of-your-face   rain.   You-can't-see-because-the-semi-passing-you-on-an-uphill-curve-is-pummeling-you-with-a-solid-wave-of-water   rain. Life-threatening rain.

I hate rain.

The sky grew dark quickly, as often it does when Mother Nature decides she is unhappy with us and wants to make her fury known. I watched for tell-tale signs of heaven liquid. A drop, a splash, on the windshield, or a line of grey coming down the mountain-side.

Something white and soft hit the windshield.

Snow? It was chilly, but I did not think Costa Rica had snow.

Another something, and another, and another stuck beneath the now-waving windshield wipers. The somethings were white, but not the bright white I lived with for years in Vermont. It was more of a grey, a light grey.

And then the darkness began to eat the sky.

Traffic slowed to a crawl. Headlights went on. Big trucks drove bumper to bumper. Our wipers could no longer keep up with the grey covering the windows and we had to deploy the washer fluid in order to see.

That was when the light came on inside my brain.

Turriabla was erupting.

Turriabla is Costa Rica's southernmost active volcano and one of its tallest. The bustling namesake town on its Caribbean slope came to mind. I stayed there in an old river-rafting lodge several times and I wondered if it was safe from the volcanic blast.

As we slowly descended from the mountains and into the central valley where the capital city, San Jose moves at almost a New York City pace, I felt both awe and mild panic roll through me. People on the roadside were wearing hospital masks. Parked cars were covered with soot several inches thick. After briefly stopping at a *soda* (small local restaurant that serves rice and beans), I learned the airport was closed due to extremely limited visibility.

But Turrialtico, my favorite river-rafting lodge was fine. No one was injured in the gas and rock explosion. However, the cloud that rose twenty-thousand feet into the air would not soon be forgotten.

31. HAMMER HEAD

He was an old man sitting on a corner in Puerto Viejo—the almost-last beach town on Costa Rica's Caribbean side. We rode through town on a tiny motorcycle and waved the first time we went by. He lifted his greying, dreadlocked head and smiled and nodded. I was a little shocked at the huge dent in his forehead. How does a person even survive the blow that must have been?

Sometimes you see a flaw or oddity on a person and even though it shocks or even disgusts you, you just put it aside and make a choice to look past it. It may not be easy because the oddity is so visible. But if you can just accept it as part of that person's journey, maybe you can appreciate the work it has done on the soul inside.

We called him Hammer Head.

He wasn't much of a shark though.

We passed him every day. Sometimes three or four times a day. He always smiled and nodded. We started stopping and Lee would call out, "Hi, Brother!" and Hammer Head would smile even bigger and ramble on in Caribbean English. I wouldn't understand most of it, but I loved the sound.

One day, we slowed as we came to the little corner where Hammer Head usually sat. It was morning and the clear air and bright sun promised the day would be hot. I was surprised to see Hammer Head on his feet. He seemed to be listing a little. Lee slowed the bike and swerved as he tried to take in the situation. Hammer Head was going down.

It was only a second before we were both off the bike. I don't know if the old Rasta man had been drinking all night or if he was having a seizure, but as he fell in slow motion it was into the arms of those who cared. A street girl nearly threw her body under him to prevent him from hitting the cement. It was a beautiful thing to see her unselfish concern. Lee reached out in time to help prevent a hard fall and several younger men caught the old man by the arms. Together they propped the him against a tree.

He seemed a little dazed, but unhurt. The street girl fluttered about him like a butterfly. She seemed to have everything under control. She was concerned, but not afraid. She assured us he would be fine.

I am still not sure what the trouble was. But, it was a beautiful thing to see such grand affection so quickly poured out on what most would think was just some lonely street guy.

We saw Hammer Head the next day and Lee called out his usual, "Hi, Brother!" The Rasta man smiled and nodded his accept-life-and-be-happy smile.

32. NICE LION

My grandson, Ayden, was a tiny three-months when we took him and his parents to Puerto Viejo, Costa Rica. His big, brown eyes stole my heart and, while Lee and I were out doing errands in the not-so-nice-town of Limon, I could not help but buy my little Squeegy a gift.

It was a stuffed lion. The super soft, I-can't-stop-touching-it-even-though-I-am-an-adult kind of lion.

We stuffed him in the big bag they gave us at the store, but he just wouldn't stay in there.

Now, keep in mind that doing errands in Limon means doing a lot of walking. Limon is the biggest port town in Costa Rica and the entire thing is the color grey. It smells like fuel. It isn't exactly safe. (And for those of you who know me, you know I go all kinds of crazy places. So if I say something isn't very safe, well....) The streets are always very busy. People walk every which way. Loud music blares from every shoe store and pharmacy. Street food is available on most every street corner—greasy fried empanadas, blackened and spicy meat on a stick, salty fried green bananas that look like thick potato chips, and *batidos*—fresh fruit smoothies that come made with water or milk and suck you in with flavors like pineapple, mango, passionfruit, guanabana, or watermelon.

So we navigated the busy streets and tried to keep Lion in the bag.

He poked his head out when we went to the Western Union window to pick up cash. We'd been there three times that morning already. We were trying to get details sorted out so we could receive a wire from home. So, there we were again, waiting in another long line. Lion wasn't very patient and kept sticking his head out of the bag to see if we were there yet and the lady behind the counter let us come up to the window early when she saw how anxious he was.

He insisted on having his own chair when we stopped to get lunch at a busy restaurant that served fried chicken, beans and rice, and salad. He wanted us to stop at the place across the street that served friend chicken, beans and rice, and salad, but he didn't get his way. So, even though he sat up nicely in his plastic chair, Lion refused to eat.

He peed on a police man.

I admit, it wasn't the best place to pee. But when Lion saw the uniform, it triggered something in his lower regions and he just had to sneak up behind the man in blue, lift his super-soft, stuffed leg and relieve himself.

An older gentleman was sitting in a wheelchair nearby, his body slumped as if it wasn't working properly. His hands were twisted and his head hung at an odd angle as if it were too heavy to hold up properly. The expression on his face was frozen as if it just wasn't able to change properly.

He must have caught Lion's inappropriate behavior out of the corner of his eye.

Slowly, the old man lifted his head. His body straightened as if it were waking up after a hundred-year nap. A silent, open-mouthed smile slowly spread across his face. His eyes lit up as if it were the 4th of July and he was six and seeing fireworks for the first time, and he laughed from the belly up. He laughed and laughed. And as we dragged lion away from the unsuspecting, now damp police man, the old man kept laughing. In fact, when we looked back a block later, he was still laughing. It was as if Rip Van Winkle had awakened from his slumber and was laughing all the lost laughs of the last hundred years.

Lion did stop misbehaving and took a nice nap while we finished running around town getting the rest of our errands done. Later that evening we introduced him to his new owner, my three-month-old, wide-eyed, blonde-haired grandson. Lion lay nicely on the floor and let Ayden pull on his ears and drool on him.

What a nice Lion.

33. TORTUGUERO

We landed on an island on Costa Rica's northern Caribbean coast. Now by island, I mean a narrow strip of land that was barely wider than the runway. The flight had been delightful, if a little shaky, in the twelve-seater plane. We were there to see a tiny hamlet called Tortuguero (place of the turtles) which was accessible only by boat or plane. I had to laugh at the airport, or lack thereof. It was a cement closet that was closed. No one greeted the plane except the water-taxi drivers that pulled up in boats to ferry us down a small portion of salt-river to the one-sidewalk town.

The brackish river that flowed through mangroves and islets was known unofficially as Costa Rica's Amazon. Home to crocodiles, caiman, river otters, manatees, and of course endangered sea turtles, it was a haven for wildlife that I couldn't wait to see.

We put our luggage on the bow of the 23ft panga and climbed in for the short ride down the river to town. Our guide pointed out a family of howler monkeys, a two-toed sloth, and some exotic birds along the way.

I love getting off the beaten path. The harder it is to get somewhere, the happier I am to get there. So when we pulled on shore and disembarked I was thrilled.

The town had a few little places to stay and we chose the oldest home on the island turned bed and breakfast. Miss Junie's. Miss Junie was the granddaughter of the original cacao plantation owner. We met her in the kitchen where, with a polka-dotted scarf covering her head, she prepped soup, greeted us in creole English, and welcomed us to her home. After a short conversation about her grandfather and the history of the place, she gave us the keys to our room. Happily, we gathered our things and climbed the wooden stairs to a balcony that stretched the entire length of the building and offered salt-river views. Our room had wood floors, a low double bed with an old quilt, and a small writing desk. It was simple enough and smelled like my grandmother's attic on a warm spring day. Off in the distance, I could hear the ocean.

I was in Heaven.

We left our bags and ate a simple lunch in the large, fancily appointed, but mostly vacant dining room and headed out to explore the town.

The sidewalk was lined with brightly colored, wooden homes. Many were on stilts to fend off any rising tide. A couple small restaurants boasted signs proclaiming fresh fish, grilled chicken, seafood soup, and local fruit. A tiny store with treasures of wood and shells and beautiful art caught my eye. I spent a few minutes touching things. A woman walked by with a bruise on her cheek and dark glasses on her face. I remember her yelling at a man across the way. Trouble is everywhere in the world these days. I wished I could have asked if she was OK. But, we turned and avoided any confrontation. Probably wise.

The town was so small it only took about a half-hour to meander the whole length of it, taking our time and looking at everything.

The weather wasn't good. By early afternoon, the rains came and we found ourselves ducking under the eaves of a restaurant. Much of Costa Rica is rain forest. The high humidity and heavy down pours create an environment of lush life. But dealing with the conditions is not always easy. We finally braved the rain and ran back to our hotel, although the running seemed pointless as I was as wet as if I had jumped fully clothed into the sea by the time I was half-way there.

I changed into something dry and settled myself on the porch under the overhang in one of the many rocking chairs. From there I watched the birds playing in the rain.

We had planned to catch a boat to Limon the next day, but the rain kept us an extra day at Miss Junie's.

I was OK with that.

It gave me the chance to chat with the workers and learn a little more about the history of the place. Miss Junie's grandfather moved there and built the grand house back in the banana glory days. He planted cacao trees everywhere, but they had since stopped producing and the entire plantation had become a refuge for endangered sea turtles with a small town supporting the endeavor.

We called the guy who made the three-hour run down the salt river to town. He said he would meet us at eight the next morning on the canal shore. He didn't make the run every day. In fact, it was hard to get hold of him. But in the end, he said he had a few other travelers who wanted to go that way. So, we agreed to leave the next morning barring any big storms.

Eight o'clock saw us with bags in hand and climbing on a narrow panga with a few other brave travelers. The sky was blue and the day promised sunshine. We left the town behind with a gentle wake following us down the broad, dark waterway.

As we left the town behind, we picked up speed. And then, much to my delight, we turned off the main throughway down a narrow winding canal. Trees canopied overhead and sunshine came through in streaks here and there as we raced along. A great white heron stood in the reeds and osprey flew overhead. When the waterway grew even narrower, our captain didn't slow a bit, but rather pushed the boat to its limits. We careened so far over as we wound around the bends that the water nearly came over the side. I trailed my fingers in the racing water and felt the sting of the spray.

At one point, the water became so shallow that we slowed almost to a stop. The captain expertly picked his way through rushes and sandbanks. A twelve-foot crocodile rested on the shore just beyond reach. And then we were off again.

I often wonder what would happened were we to have had a dramatic engine failure an hour-and-a-half into our trip. It wouldn't be my first experience with engine failure hours from civilization. I would like to believe the captain would just call one of his buddies on the cell phone. But, even with all our modern technology these days, you never know.

We finally came to the mouth of the river and stopped to watch a flock of egrets walking in the sand.

There is something fantastic about being far away from the bustle of humanity.

As we came into Limon, I was shocked back into the rat-race by the appearance of huge tankers, rusted metal warehouses, and crumbling cement office buildings. What a contrast.

I adjusted my mind to fend off the sickening feeling of man kind's pollution of our glorious earth. I love people, I love the workers down by the docks, I love the dirty-faced kids and the moms who are struggling to raise children alone. I just wish I could put these two parts—the beauty of the earth and the beauty of the people—together in a way that honored both.

34. WITCHES

The moon was full and the sky was warm and cloudy. Not many stars twinkled in the night sky. Lee and I sat under the drifting clouds at the Cool and Calm Cafe across from the beach at the end of the road. Cool and Calm is in a little town that is accessible only by one long, straight road that runs through an old chocolate plantation and it really is the end of the road. When you drive through town, the road turns to sand. It runs along the beach until it comes to the mouth of a little river. There, on the near side of the river bank, is an old hand-painted sign that reads, "The end of the road." Get out of your car and cross the river and you will find yourself hiking through the rain forest and into Panama.

The witches were out.

OK, maybe you fancy yourself a witch, and if you do I mean no offense. If you are a witch, perhaps you will understand the odd feeling of that evening better than I.

We were hanging out at the tiny café which was owned by our good friend Andy. Andy, a Rasta, lost a leg in an earthquake accident back in the 90s. The earthquake was so powerful that it sunk an island just over the border in Panama. We'd been at the cafe most of the afternoon and into the evening. Our lobster was history and we were sipping cocktails and listening to real calypso played on a small guitar, a set of hand drums, and a bass made from a long stick, an equally long string, and an upside-down barrel. I wish I could have recorded the slinging harmonies and earthy sound. It was a gift to me.

About 9:00 pm the women rode in. There were nine of them.

They rode up from the surf and through the palms on horses. Andy told us that they came every full moon, stayed for a drink, and rode off again. They tied their mounts to the palm trees surrounding a cement picnic-table sitting in the sand and then swarmed the small restaurant in a quiet fashion, talking gingerly among themselves. They sat at several of the small wooden tables and ordered drinks.

Lee and I vacated our space, drinks still in hand. Normally we would have stayed and chatted, but it appeared these women did not want any interruption and the energy of the place radically changed. We walked across the street and found ourselves gravitating toward the horses.

They were so still.

I cautiously approached an older chestnut and she did not whinny or shift her hooves or even flick her ears. In my experience, horses are never really still and they are almost always nervous when strangers approach. The behavior of this creature completely baffled me. Lee approached a taller, younger grey. Same thing, not a twitch.

It was as if a spell had been cast over the animals that almost prevented them from being aware of us at all.

We settled ourselves at the table in the center of the horse ring and talked quietly while the ladies sipped their cocktails across the street. They weren't long, maybe a half-hour, and the energy changed again as they rose from their tables, fiddled with their checks, and said goodbye to Andy. As they moved out of the cafe and back toward the horses, we moved further out onto the dark beach. Scattered moonlight played among the waves turning the surf to a glow-in-the-dark white.

Without much ado, the women swung onto their unearthly mounts, rode past us into the moonlit waves, and galloped down the beach, wind whipping hair and clothing and churning hooves throwing up spray. They galloped away from town, away from the last vestiges of civilization, and toward miles of deserted beach into the night.

35. RASTA ANDY

Andy had one leg. He lost his other leg when a wall fell on him during the great earthquake of 1994, the one that sunk an entire island beneath the sea. Andy was my friend. He owned a little beach restaurant called the Cool and Calm Cafe. It was across the road from Manzanillo Beach at the end of the road in Costa Rica.

Andy's restaurant served coconut rice and whole red snapper or fresh lobster with curried vegetables and, of course, rum. The lobster was a bit expensive—twelve dollars, I think—but I bought it because one-legged Andy free-dived for it himself. Well, until he had a bad accident.

I had not seen Andy in probably a month and, when I walked into his little rustic restaurant, I found him sitting in a wheel chair. His dreads were a little longer. His beautiful black face was a little pinched—he obviously was in some pain—but he still wore that every-little-thing-gonna-be-alright air. When I asked him what happened, he explained about the accident and the pins in his leg in an easy fashion and without complaint.

The sand entry to Andy's little eatery had been washed away by rain and time and it wasn't exactly easy for Andy and his wheelchair to navigate. So we hired two big boys, a wheelbarrow, and several shovels. And we went to work moving sand from the beach to the front door of the Cool and Calm Cafe. We paid the boys in *plata* (cash) and a few cans of the local *cervasa.* A few hours later, Andy had the level entrance he needed to get to work.

Andy took it all in stride. He thanked us in a simple fashion and seemed to add the change of circumstances to his life folder. It was as if everything in life was to simply be accepted. I admired his ability to take life in stride.

A month later Andy was up and walking again. He was still unable to use his prosthetic leg and needed crutches. But, he was upright. When I asked him how he was feeling, he gave me very little complaint. I stopped to reflect on how this kind Rasta man had endured the loss of one leg and now was slowly recovering from—of all things—the near ruin of his other leg, and yet he never seemed to complain.

Oh, I forgot to mention, the first time I met Andy, he was riding a bicycle. Yes, a one-legged man riding a regular bicycle. A one-legged man riding a bicycle and free-diving for lobster and running a Cool and Calm Cafe on the beach at the end of the road in Costa Rica.

So, I guess from the beginning, I was amazed.

36. MR.SUGAR

We called him Mr. Sugar. It wasn't his real name, but we didn't know his real name. At least not for the first few weeks.

He stood in the middle of the road just where you pass Maxi's restaurant and the road turns into the beach and continues until you reach the sign that says, "The end of the road."

Mr. Sugar often stood in the middle of the road. He stood there wearing a bright, orange vest. It may have been a life-vest, but he wasn't planning to get in a boat. He was there to wave you through, or help you park your car, or direct your walking, or anything else he thought you might need.

He was in no way an official anything.

The first time I saw Mr. Sugar, he was frantically waving his arms. I was confused. He obviously was directing me to do something, but I had no idea what. All his waving didn't seem to be in any particular direction and I thought he might be trying to get me to stop for an emergency right there on the beach. But, the only thing I could see that was demanding attention was the turquoise sea and the foamy white waves.

The second time I saw Mr. Sugar—again directing traffic in the middle of the road—we were driving past and Lee stopped the car to talk to him. Mr. Sugar babbled on about people and beaches and I really could not understand what he was saying. I thought maybe it was his broken Caribbean English.

The third time I saw Mr. Sugar, we were walking and we stopped to say, "Hi." This time, the wiry Creole man spoke as if he had a degree in Literature. His English was educated and perfectly clear.

We had a conversation with him and discovered his name was Socrates.

I am learning to reserve judgement.

Everyone in town said Mr. Sugar was crazy. Harmless, but crazy. And maybe he was. But, after spending a few minutes getting to know him, I tried hard, every time I passed him, to listen to what he had to say. He was a gentle soul and I wanted to hear his story. He obviously wanted to help people or he wouldn't have stood, dressed in a bright orange life-jacket, providing free traffic direction all day.

Which reminds me of the week of the festival. Poor Socrates. There was traffic everywhere. Cars lined the beach until there was nowhere left to park. Tents were set up in every available space and tens of thousands of people flocked from all over the country. Mr. Sugar was beside himself. He waved frantically and pointed and spun in circles and tried to direct everything until he was so overwhelmed he gave up and went and sat on a park bench.

You know, maybe Mr. Sugar was crazy. Maybe his mind was scattered. And maybe directing traffic gave him a little bit of that everything-is-right-with-the-world feeling. Maybe it helped him take control of his own internal, confusing world.

Hmmm...

Maybe we all should be directing traffic.

37. PORTAL ON THE BEACH

It was a tree fork. Like a fork in the road, but made from a tree, or a branch from a tree. And lying on the beach.

It was huge—much larger than me—and heavy.

Lee thought we should lift it up and bury its ends in the sand like a giant upside down Y.

So we did.

We dragged it up the beach until it was above the high-tide mark. We spun it so it was facing the water. And then we dug two holes, one for each leg of the inverted Y.

We tried to lift it, but were unsuccessful getting it to stand.

That was when we noticed people watching.

A local Costa Rican boy came over and started digging.

Then a middle-aged touristy lady came over and helped us lift.

A local man enjoying the beach with his family added his strength to the production, and soon we had the tree fork standing upside down. An arch. Or possibly, a gateway.

Solemnly, we took turns walking through it.

I am not sure where it led, but without common words, we all understood it led somewhere.

PANAMA

38. PICTURE THIS: OUT ISLAND

What's it like to live on an island? And I don't mean a touristy island with cute little shops and restaurants. I mean an island with no roads where the houses are accessible only by boat.

Picture this:

You cross the channel in your 23ft panga in three to four foot waves. It's raining. The rain stings your face. You are drenched to the bone. As you near the island, the shallow water is so clear that, even in the rain, you can see the starfish and coral on the bottom. You pull up at the dilapidated dock and tie off, trying to allow for changing tides and making sure the bilge pump is working so the boat doesn't fill with water and sink. Then you grab your grocery bags and dodge through the trees to the golf cart which is locked with a stainless steel cable to a tree. You unlock the cable, throw your stuff in the basket on the back of the golf cart, pull up the seat, use a wrench to spark the engine to life and try not to burn yourself in the process, put the seat back down, jump on, grab the wire between your feet that bypasses the accelerator that doesn't work, and practically throw yourself out of the seat as you give it too much gas. Then you pull even harder on the accelerator wire to give the cart enough oomph to get up the stony path to your house. As you come around that last curve, you bounce on your seat frantically to try to get the wheels to get enough traction in the slick, red mud so you don't end up spinning your tires and getting stuck in a precarious predicament.

You thankfully reach the crest of the hill and glide effortlessly down onto your manicured lawn. Then you park the golf cart with both of its front tires against heavy rocks since there is no parking-brake and you really don't want to chase it down the hill.

You can hear the dogs barking inside.

You fumble for your keys in the rain, trying not to get your clothes too dirty with the red clay you now have on your hands. As you turn the key in the lock, both dogs come shooting out past you and then stop in their tracks like they forgot who they were so excited to see. They realize their error, turn around, and jump all over you.

You walk into the high-ceilinged living room that smells like wood and has a cool breeze blowing through the glassless-screen-in only windows and you throw your heavy load on the tile counter-top in the kitchen. Then you strip down to nothing and go find some dry clothes. Ah... Relief.

The rain is pounding on the roof. The dogs are settled back in their favorite spots, and you sit on the wicker couch, put up your feet, and turn on the TV that blabbers on at you in comforting Spanish that you barely understand. Fifteen minutes go by while you catch your breath.

Then you drag yourself into the kitchen where you look out over the jungle and into the backyard. A flooded stream rushes by. You can hear the parrots squawking in the trees. The rain must be almost over.

You pull salmon, mangoes, and blue cheese out of the grocery bags along with a fresh jar of coconut oil and a few green onions. You boil some rice and gently cook the salmon in coconut oil and onions. Then you peel a mango, heat it in the yummy stuff in the bottom of the fish-pan, pour it out onto the fish, and top the whole thing with blue cheese.

After licking your fingers when you've finished your meal, you wash the dishes by hand, careful with the water even though you know the tanks must be full from the day's rain. The down-pour slows to a pitter-patter as the sun sets out over the water and you light incense and put it in all the corners of the room as the bugs begin to squash themselves through the screens. You turn on one low light and try to read a book for a bit, but the beetles that are attracted by the light buzz your head like fighter jets. So, you shut off the light and retire early. A big, lazy fan creates a cool breeze in your room as you slip under a light cotton blanket and you drift off the sleep listening to the crickets and the drip of left-over rain.

It's all about the mix isn't it? The struggle and the work and the peace and the beauty. The knowing that if you forgot something at the store it will have to wait days until you are ready to brave the waves again and the clean smell of rain-watered grass and warm sun in the morning. The beauty lies in the contrast.

39. NO BUENO

No Bueno is not exactly the kind of name you want to call someone. But he seemed to like it. It wasn't his real name, of course. His name was Carlos and he was a Ngobe Indian who lived with his family on the remote island of Solarte in Bocas Del Toro, Panama. To get there from the USA you would have to fly into Panama City, take a small plane to the airport on Isla Colon and then take a boat from there. Solarte has no roads. There is a sidewalk in the Ngobe village, but most of the homes are accessible only by boat. We lived up on the hill for about six months. It was a nice gig, although the bugs were unbelievable. The home was big and open and had screens on the windows, but no glass. Wind blew through all day and big lazy fans kept the place cool.

We bought a panga, a 23ft traditional boat with an 85hp motor on it. We named her after my dog, Babygirl. She was our car (the panga, not the dog). There was no sense in owning a car in the islands and the panga was a necessity. I loved her. She was reliable and fast. I loved shooting across the bay, wind in my hair, skipping over the ocean. Sometimes I was afraid we might hit the coral beneath us because the water was so clear and it had that swimming pool effect—the one where the water is ten feet deep but it feels like you can reach out and touch the bottom.

We had a place to park her. An overhang at the Rock Dock. Rock Dock was the name of the dilapidated concrete dock a quarter mile below the house. At one time it was used to haul in supplies from the ferry, but years of wind and salt eroded it into a withering strip of stones and rebar.

Nothing lasts long in the islands.

Non-the-less, it was enough. We had a nice overhang to keep most of the rain out of the boat, which was a good thing because we had no bilge pump and a night of rain could sink a boat.

Then there were the Indians.

The Ngobe don't make a lot of money. For the most part that is OK since they own land and build homes from wild hardwoods, palms, and bamboo. But they have the opinion that we Gringos have more money than we need, so once in a while they take something useful and figure it isn't a problem because we can replace it and they can't.

Enter Babygirl.

And No Bueno.

No Bueno was a good guy. He was short with milked-coffee colored skin and lovely dark-rimmed eyes that looked like he was always wearing heavy eye-liner. He was fair and jovial and drove a taxi boat—a panga just like ours. Mostly, he drove for Bambooda—the off-the-grid hostel just down the shore from us. But he also drove school-boat. No, not school-bus. School-boat.

The kids came down from their houses in the jungle on the hill. They walked down narrow, muddy paths past crocodile infested rivers (OK, that sounds terrible. There were non-aggressive caimans in the streams.) down to the dock. They wore crisp, white shirts and navy-blue skirts or trousers and they all arrived at the Rock Dock brand-spanking clean. In all honesty, I don't know how their mothers kept their clothes so clean. I suppose it had something to do with scrubbing them on the rocks. I can't get my whites white for nothing. Maybe I should go visit with the Ngobe and take a laundry lesson.

Laundry aside...

The kids came down to the dock and No Bueno took them by boat to the main island where they attended school.

So of course, No Bueno was very careful with his boat. Not careful driving it, although he was that too. He was careful locking everything up so stuff wouldn't be stolen—like a motor, or a gas tank, or an expensive hose connecting the two.

He understood the problem with the Indians.

After all, he was one.

Which brings me to how No Bueno got his name.

We had just moved into the house on the hill and Babygirl had just been purchased. (The boat, not the dog. The dog was adopted off the streets in Mexico, but that is an entirely different story.) We sped across the water to the Rock Dock all excited and full of enthusiasm for our new adventure in island living.

We pulled up to the crumbling dock, jumped out, and tied off through secure looking places between stones and wood with our new blue lines.

Carlos (later known as No Bueno) pulled up right behind us. He had finished his school-boat run and was headed up to his house in the jungle. He shut off his engine, removed the key from the ignition, and took a line of thick cable and ran it around a non-removable part of the dock, through the handle on his gas tank, through a bracket on the motor, through a drilled hole in the fiberglass on his panga, and back up to the non-removable part of the dock. Then he locked the whole thing with a padlock the size of my fist.

When he was finished, he climbed up onto the dock, took a quick look at our bright blue, nicely tied lines and said, "No bueno."

And off he went up the muddy path and into the jungle.

Lee and I just stood there looking at each other. Apparently, our nice new lines were not going to do the trick.

This is where the story becomes like *The Three Little Pigs* or *Goldilocks and the Three Bears*. You know, one of those stories where the same event is repeated over and over again with just a small change each time. And each time the answer is...

"No bueno."

Wind out of our sails, we hesitantly left Babygirl by herself and trudged up the muddy hill to our house. (The golf cart which had earlier been driven into the sea by one of the adorable little Ngobe kids had not yet been Jimmy-rigged.) From Carlos' expression and short declaration, we were under the distinct impression we had better not leave Babygirl alone long.

Up at the house, we plundered the bodega for a length of cable and a padlock. Actually, I was amazed we found them. In a normal world, you wouldn't just walk into the house a find ten feet of stainless steel cable and a brand new padlock WITH the key. But then this was not a normal world.

We slid back down the hill and secured the boat. Well, sort of. The cable wasn't long enough to do all the under and over Carlos did. But we did manage to run it through a bracket on the motor, around one of the poles on the bimini, and back to the dock.

Just at that moment, Carols reappeared, apparently done with lunch and ready to go back to work. He quickly glanced at our handy work.

"No bueno," was all he said and he was off again.

Not having the energy to bang back over the waves to the hardware store, we decided to risk leaving Babygirl not-too-securely-cabled and we spent the rest of that day and that night on the island. But, we were up early scooting across the channel to the big island where we bought a longer piece of cable.

Carlos magically seemed to reappear right when, after running the cable through everything we could possibly imagine, we were clicking our brand new little pad lock into place.

"No bueno."

Maddening? Funny? I wasn't sure which. But the message was loud and clear.

So, we bought a new, bigger lock.

"No bueno."

We bought a thicker piece of cable figuring maybe ours was too easy to cut through with a pair of wire snippers.

"No bueno."

That was about the time we actually started calling him No Bueno, behind his back of course because he really was a nice guy and was just trying to help. He knew his own people better than we did and he knew what they were capable of.

But after doing everything we could possibly think of to secure our little Babygirl, we still got the inevitable,

"No bueno."

We finally figured it out the night our fuel line was stolen.

Apparently is wasn't enough to just lock everything to everything in an OCD manner and secure everything with a lock big enough to guard Fort Knox. Apparently the line connecting the fuel tank to the motor actually needed to be removed and taken home each and every evening.

It cost $107 US dollars to replace.

No Bueno is a nice guy.

I like him. I like his family. And when his sister hobbled down from the jungle every day to go by boat to the hospital for physical therapy for her knee, I always asked how she was doing.

I still think No Bueno has the coolest, eye-liner rimmed eyes.

And the day we passed him on the water, us in Babygirl and he in his boat, and I enthusiastically waved and accidently hollered, "Hola! No Bueno!"... he smiled.

I have no idea what was going through his head, but the name stuck and he didn't seem to mind.

Maybe he was just gloating in an I-told-you-so kind of way after we forked out the cash for a new fuel line.

Maybe he just liked the name.

40. JACK SPARROW

Jack Sparrow doesn't have any teeth—any upper teeth that is. His wrinkled black face seems to take on a life of its own as he gets just a little too close to you and smiles, eyes bright and body in constant motion. His English is colored by *Guari Guari*—a local Caribbean Patios that makes his sing-song voice a little difficult to understand.

Every time I inadvertently get close to him, he grabs my hand and begins to read my palm.

One day he told me I would travel soon, that I would go and see my family. Truthfully, I had been turning the idea over in my mind, wanting to visit my youngest son for a few days.

Another time, he told me I was too controlling. Not what I really wanted to here, but truthful never-the-less. He told me I worry too much and need to relax, and he was right. The need to control comes from fear that things are not going to be OK.

In fact, every time Jack Sparrow gets hold of my hand, truth pours from his wrinkled lips.

"You love Jesus very much," he said to me one day. "Come closer to Him," he instructed me. "Bless you, bless you," he said.

Finally, I asked Jack Sparrow why he does what he does.

"It is all for Jesus," he replied.

In my world palm reading and Jesus do not go together. They have always been at direct odds with each other.

I gave Jack a dollar so he could get something to eat. He bowed his head low and thanked me with gummed Guari Guari words and gentle humility.

Who am I to judge? Jack Sparrow may just be the closet things to Jesus on these dirty streets.

41. SAIGON DOGS

My lovely daughter, Sarah, and her two-year-old moon child, Ayden, came to visit me in Panama. We were so thrilled to have them and wanted to show them the islands, so we put everybody in the panga and headed out into the blue. After skirting the main island, we pulled into a little glassy cove called Saigon Bay.

Saigon Bay is rimmed with houses—some built on docks not anchored to land, but rather to mangroves and accessible only by boat. The water is clear and shallow and starfish are abundant.

We putted along for a while, dipping our fingers in the warm Caribbean and peering at the seagrass and life below, until, after some begging on my part, Lee shut off the motor so we could just drift.

Everything was peaceful but for the two dogs barking in the distance.

Little Ayden leaned over the side and tried to grab the starfish. I opened a bottle of water and sipped a little while dragging my other hand in the sea, just letting the liquid run though my fingers.

We only floated for a couple of minutes. There was more current than we expected and the dogs' barking was incessant and a little annoying. So, Lee turned the key to start the engine.

Nothing.

That's the moment you take everything in to see just what you are up against.

The dogs were on the deck of one of those only-accessible-by-water houses and no one appeared to be home. They were very big dogs. Very big pit bulls. The water was shallow—shallow enough to stand in—but spiny, black sea urchins dotted the sea floor. (Funny how you notice starfish when everything is calm and lovely and you notice sea urchins when you feel yourself slipping into trouble.)

We had no paddle in the boat. We lost it a week earlier and had not taken the time to replace it.

We had a small anchor we'd just purchased at an impromptu boat lawn-sale.

We had my two-year-old grandson on board.

Lee began getting a little desperate in his attempts to start the motor as we drifted rather rapidly toward the dogs. The current was playing that trick on you where it drags you in the only direction you really don't want to go.

I threw the anchor, but all it did was drag on the sea floor. I pulled it in and threw it again and again, jerking it hard each time trying to get it to set with no avail.

Sarah held Ayden.

The dogs, seeing us drifting ever closer, began to get themselves in a real tizzy. Slobber was visibly noticeable.

When things get really bad, I slip into this weird calm. My thinking gets really clear and my movement gets very fluid. It became obvious we were going to hit the deck and there was nothing we could do to stop it.

No one was home to prevent the slathering monsters from having their way with us.

Bump...

The fiberglass boat hit the wooden deck. A sickening feeling hit my stomach.

I remained as calm as possible, knowing any sign of fear or aggression would only inflame the dogs.

The pit bull closest to us was massive. His coat dirty white was marred with dark brown spots. He was beside himself, pacing on the dock just inches from the boat. Lee could not risk using his hand to push us away. So he desperately looked for anything long-handled he could use to push us back out into open water. The only thing he could find was a machete.

Normally you wouldn't carry a machete in your boat, but this was Panama. And in Panama, a machete can come in handy for a variety of things such as cutting a path through the jungle, chopping off coconut tops to get at the sweet water inside or, in this case, pushing your boat away from the dock to avoid being eaten by pit bulls.

Unfortunately, the pit bulls were familiar with machetes.

They went berserk.

Lee quickly stashed the machete out of sight so he wouldn't antagonize the dogs further, and he did the only other thing he could think of. He jumped in the water.

It seemed to distract the huge white dog a little.

Lee struggled through the sea urchin forest to the bow of the boat. I would love to say he ran, but it is impossible to run in chest deep water. I threw him the bow-line and he pulled us away from the dock just as the slobber-flinging dog had regained his composure and was trying to figure out how to jump in the boat, now that Lee was not in his way.

In slow motion, like a scene from a movie, Lee pulled us from danger.

Sarah was in shock, holding Ayden tight, her eyes bright with fear.

A half-built home stood on stilts in the water next door. It was accessible only by boat, or by swimming if the dogs chose to take the plunge. Thankfully, they seemed afraid of the water. We tied off to the unfinished house and took a minute to take stock of the situation.

"It's OK, Sarah," I said to my daughter who was still wide-eyed and barely moving. "We may still be in a bit of a pickle, but we are out of danger now."

I had phone numbers of water-taxi guys that could come get us if we could not get the engine started. But Lee, with a moment of relative calm to take a look at the problem, was soon able to get the motor started.

As we sailed away across the open bay, Sarah, with Ayden safely in her lap, said the most unexpected thing to me.

"So, Mom, when are you going to write your book?"

42. THE BOCAS TRIANGLE

We took the panga down the coast of Isla San Cristobal, through the mangroves, and into Dolphin Bay. From there we navigated through the cut by the teak trees and all the way to the mainland where a mechanic lived in a house in the water, well not really IN the water, in the mangroves and ON the water, actually ON the water. It was a long ride from Bocas Town—about forty minutes—but, it was well rewarded with the elusive engine part we were looking for. Finally, the starter on the panga was fixed.

There was a tiny gas station next to the mechanic's house, but we decided we not to fill up. Well, Lee decided not to fill up. He said we had enough gas to get home. Storm clouds were brewing and he wanted to try to beat the rain.

After backtracking out of the bay, we raced through the mangroves. Dark thunderheads spread across the sky.

Leaving the mangroves behind, we headed north and kept the island close on our left. The rain began and visibility plummeted. We figured we would be OK if we hugged the island until it ended. From there we should be able to see Bocas Town.

We were wrong.

The rain was coming in torrents and we couldn't see Bocas. So we headed at a ten-degree angle and kept San Cristobal behind us and to the left. It was a short crossing and Bocas should come into view quickly, even in the heaviest rain. I felt confident with San Cristobal over my shoulder as a landmark. We would be fine.

The rain stung my face and the waves were high. The crossing was not exactly fun and the only thing I was really worried about was driving into the wind without much gas. The rough conditions would make for bad mileage.

After pounding along for five minutes, land came into view. My first reaction was relief, knowing that, if we did run out of gas, there would be someone around to give us a tow. But as we drew closer to what we assumed was Bocas Town, I quickly realized that the land did not look familiar at all.

About that time, I lost San Cristobal to the mist.

It is a very unsettling feeling to be staring at islands that look nothing like they should when you are almost out of gas and it's raining really hard.

We drew a little closer to the islands. They were small and dotted the surface of the sea. Our gas was running dangerously low. (I'm talking fumes.) So, it seemed the only sensible thing to do was to shut off the engine and drift for a while until the rain cleared and visibility improved. The mountains of the main land would give us our bearings again, if only we could see them.

So we shut off the motor and drifted.

The boat didn't get any closer to or further away from the small islands. It drifted in a circle. Very strange behavior for a boat.

I took stock of our water supply and checked out our one small bag of peanuts. Not much, but enough to get us through until the weather cleared.

That was when Lee spotted the sailboat. It was anchored between two tiny islands.

There are a lot of deserted sailboats in the area. So, there was no guarantee anyone would be on board. But we opted to use a little more gas fumes and check it out.

We pulled alongside the 40ft craft and called.

I thought I heard a voice below deck.

Lee called again and we were greeted by a wiry, old sailor and his plump and happy wife.

Relief.

They even had gas, gas mixed with two-cycle oil, the kind we needed.

Almost a miracle

But the really weird part came when we asked where Bocas Town was and they pointed to a strip of land so far off in the distance we could hardly see it, even though the sky was finally clearing. Not only was it incredibly far away, it was in the complete wrong direction.

There is simply no way for me to explain how we got to where we were.

We know the area well. We had lived in Bocas for nearly two years and had explored everywhere with the panga. The place we found ourselves was a half-hour ride from Bocas in the opposite direction on a good day. Even if we could have somehow gotten turned around, which was impossible because we kept San Cristobal on our left the whole way, there was no way we had enough gas to get where to we were. Then there was the extra half-hour of lost time we would have added to our trip. And that through rough seas.

I have re-christened Bocas Del Toro, *The Bocas Triangle*.

We thanked our rescuers, added the gas to our tank, and sped home

133

with the lifting rain.

We talked for hours that evening about what happened. Bocas Triangle, definitely.

PS,

The morning after our bizarre dis-and-re-appearance, I was approached in the street by a good friend and local, my favorite jungle man, William. He heard we got lost. He knew what was going on. He had it happen to him on several occasions.

William explained in his perfect Caribbean English that a bad pirate spirit stayed in the area when the big ships came and killed the Indians and stole the gold. He was talking about Christopher Columbus who was not the good guy we were taught he was but ransacked the islands and left a lot of blood on the ground.

"Take off your shirt," William instructed. "The pirate spirit will lasso you. But, if you take off your shirt and turn it inside out and put it back on and then turn around three times, you will find your way back home."

I used to think such advice was the remnant of children's fairy tales. Now I am not so sure.

William also said his grandfather told him about a big ship that was fully lit and came to offer lost people help late in the evening. He warned us to never accept the help or they would take us very far away.

PPS,

The very next day we got a distress call from our friend, Stewart. It was late in the day. The sun was setting and black storm clouds had settled in. Lightening was blazing in the distance. Stewart was in his motor-less sailboat and the wind was uncooperative. He could not get home. Could we come in our panga and give him a tow?

Problem? He seemed very confused and could not really describe where he was.

We braved the storm and the thickening darkness, but we could not find him.

It was just too dangerous for us to continue looking for him, especially when he had no idea where he was. So, we headed back to our sailboat in the harbor and called Stewart to recommend he drop anchor and wait until morning. He was panicking. So, we set out again, but the night was so black we could not see a thing except when the lightening lit the sky. We decided it would be safer to find one of the local Indian boaters. They are better equipped than we in difficult conditions and might be able to find our friend. The local guy sped off just as heaven opened and the rain came down so hard I could not even keep my eyes open, much less see.

With the help of a few lights from nearby ships, we found our way safely back to our sailboat. An hour later Stewart's boat was towed in.

In the morning the story we heard sounded awfully familiar. Stewart had been in one place one moment and far, far away the next.

Pirate spirits?

I don't have a better explanation.

43. JERRY

I stepped out of the grocery store into the dark street and found Jerry standing before me with a plastic bag in his hand.

Lee, who stood beside me asked, "You been shopping?"

Jerry opened the bag and inside was a wheel. A small, hard rubber wheel. It was for his shopping cart.

I had seen Jerry cleaning in the park and along the streets many times. I often thanked him for working so hard. Bocas isn't exactly clean and it was always nice to see someone working to make it a little better.

I didn't know Jerry wasn't working for the town. I had no idea he was doing it for free.

I did know he carried clothing in his shopping cart, along with his broom and dust pan, and an old lamp he was planning to fix.

I also knew he carried his Bible. I usually saw him with it stuffed in the pocket of his shorts.

Once I saw him sitting on a park bench early in the morning, reading.

Lee didn't see the ever-present Bible, so he asked, "Do you have your Bible?"

Jerry's eyes lit up and a smile jumped to his previously serious face.

He patted his pocket. It was hiding there, well cared for and protected as the most valuable thing he carried.

I decided keep an eye out for Jerry. Next time I saw him cleaning, I thanked him for his hard work and I took him out to lunch.

It was a privilege to eat with a man who loves God and loves to clean.

44. LUCIFER AND THE ENGINE

Jerry is homeless. He lives on the streets and the beach on Isla Colon in the tropical island chain of Bocas Del Toro, Panama. I really like Jerry. He is a gentle soul who spends hours every day cleaning the streets even though no one asked, and certainty no one pays him.

I sat on the street with Jerry one night, late and in the rain. He sat on his piece of cardboard and I sat on the hard tile just outside a Chino (Bocas-ease for grocery store. They are all owned by Chinese). The long over-hang protected us easily from the rain and we talked.

Jerry was born in Colon, the city that guards the Panama Canal on the Caribbean side. It is notorious for violent crime. When he was born, his mother dedicated him to Lucifer. He explained that when he was very small, he was killed many times, shot mostly. He explained that every time he died, he just got back up. It seemed an unpleasant memory for him. He asked me how many times I died, as if it was just normal for people to die and then get up again. Of course, I told him I had never died.

Jerry told me that when he was old enough, he studied witchcraft for three years. He studied so he would have the tools he needed to be a drug trafficker. He talked some about Mexico and a boat headed to England that never got there and Columbians that were impressed with the magic he could do. He explained that he could turn a snake into a chain and back again and that he could turn a cigarette into a hundred-dollar bill, but he didn't like to make money that way because every time he did, he paid for it with a year of his life.

I sat listening to the rain and trying to decipher everything Jerry said. He sat mostly with his head bowed, his black dread locks hanging in his face. Occasionally he looked directly at me, his black eyes piercing. He switched back and forth from English to Spanish and I dared not interrupt him to ask him to repeat himself lest I interrupt the flow of his story.

I had known Jerry for several months. I'd bought him coffee and lunch. He never asked for money. In fact, he told me he had money. He just didn't have access to it. He showed me the Bible he had tucked into a backpack that was stashed in the bottom of the shopping cart he pushed around town. He talked about "the engine," but every time he mentioned it, he lost me.

That night, as I sat listening to him in the rain, I finally figured out that "the engine" was a spirit that lived with him. Jerry often told me what "the engine" thought about things. And as he spoke of his time running cocaine, he frequently threw in side comments about this ever present companion.

So I asked Jerry about the engine.

"It's a very bad spirit," he said.

I must say, my head was reeling. I read a book once about a man who did some mission work in Africa and ran into stories similar to Jerry's. I found the stories fascinating. I think when we feel strongly pulled to something, it comes to us. And I think my time in Panama was evidence of that. I was learning a little about, not just Jerry, but the under-belly of the third world country I was living in.

"Other people have a face just like me," Jerry said as he pulled out two forms of ID so I could see his picture. Was he referring to shape shifters? People who could mimic someone else?

"There are ships here that fly like planes, but look like big balls of fire," he said. "They fly into Costa Rica."

I had my own thoughts about aliens and Costa Rica and even the possibility of the Illuminati (the not-so-secret-anymore group of rich elite who are running the world) using Costa Rica and its vast unpeopled land as a base for operations and a safe zone in case of total world chaos.

"There are aliens here," Jerry explained. "But, they are just here to learn."

He explained that if we were nice to them, they would be nice to us. They had no bad intentions. They were just studying mankind.

"There is a hole in the sea," he told me. "A place where they hid the gold. The spirits protect it."

I added this to my information about the bad pirate spirit we evidently encountered when we were lost at sea.

Jerry didn't have a computer. He never watched TV. I didn't think this was the kind of stuff he would just make up. And the way he talked was like a long, thoughtful ramble—almost more like he was remembering and talking to himself than talking to me.

I stopped Jerry occasionally in his ramble to ask a few clarifying questions.

Was he a powerful witch?

Not really, he just knew enough to get by.

Were there other witches in Bocas?

Yes, many. Everyone knew it, but no one talked about it. In fact, he said that Bocas was "full of devils."

Did he have to go back and start life out as a baby again every time he died?

No, he just got up and kept going.

Did other people in Bocas traffic drugs?

Yes, many of the people who looked poor actually had tons of money stashed in their houses, but they lived simply so no one would be aware.

It was so late—after 1:00 am—and I was involuntarily yawning. Finally, I had to excuse myself and go get some sleep. Could we talk more in the morning?

Yes, he would be happy to talk to me. But, I was not to tell anyone about the witches.

I left him there on his cardboard, sheltered from the rain. I still had questions to ask. My curiosity was on fire. I went to bed with thoughts racing through my head. In my time in Central America, I have sometimes felt like an anthropologist, a discoverer of stories and faces, a documenter of ambitions and fears, an observer of authentic life.

I thought I ran away to Mexico when my husband died. I thought I ran away from pain, from truth. But I think maybe I was led away to find life in the dark places of humanity, to find the beauty of the poor people, and to expose it.

45. THE CURSE OF JACKAROO

Jackaroo was a sailboat. She was sleek and sporty and, by rumor, had been around the world twice. We bought her and moved in. We polished all the teak and scrubbed the white leather, and recovered the stateroom bed in silver and hung slate curtains and threw bright green pillows and rugs everywhere.

She was a gem.

We bought her for a song. They said she would never run again. But, we discovered the brutality of a prospective buyer whose offer was denied because of its offensive low-balling. He pulled the panel off the back of the dash and pulled out all of the wires. No wonder she wouldn't start! There was no problem with the engine. She purred like a kitten. Our risk paid off and our new home on the water was ready to set sail again.

But it didn't last.

In a few short months, we were snared by the lure of another beauty. A 60 foot, one of a kind William Garden design. She was opulent and alluring. Hand-hewn teak adorned her every inch. Pillars guarded her galley. Wide stairs complete with a landing promoted her entry. Gentle, floral carvings surrounded the beveled mirror in her lovers' nest. Brass clocks and windows spoke of rings on her fingers. Her wide decks beckoned sunbathers.

We fell in love.

And so we threw Jackaroo aside.

And she wasn't happy.

We had lavished so much attention on her, including taking her out of the water and spending countless hours painting her hull and repairing all the ravages of time. We oiled the teak on her rear deck and bleached the shining white non-skid surface of her bow. We took down her sails and carefully washed them and inspected them for signs of wear. We oiled her hardworking engine and replaced worn seals. But we decided we would not be the ones to reap the benefits of all that attention and we put her up for sale.

We advertised. We sent out word around the world that Jackaroo was for sale. Calls came in from Australia and Costa Rica and South Africa and Canada and the USA. People bought plane tickets and flew to our tiny island in the Caribbean.

But most of them never arrived.

An eco-farmer from Costa Rica lost acres of his four-hundred acre farm to a forest fire. A widow from Canada broke her foot and was left stranded in her travels. A carny from Australia discovered his son was kidnapped. A retired businessman from California fell ill and was hospitalized.

And then the break-ins began.

The first time, they drilled a pin hole in the lock, took off the door, ravaged the cabin as though they were looking for something, and then carefully replaced the door and the lock. We could not find a thing missing. The second time, they took the silver blanket and two hats. Again, they carefully replaced the door as if no one had been there. Then a prospective buyer, an intrepid traveler who finally made his way past whatever hound guarded the gate to our island, arrived. He was

143

scheduled to see Jackaroo at ten o'clock. We were excited because he was excited. We were exhausted from the strangeness and anxious to hand her over to a new owner.

But they came again. Whoever was breaking in and not taking anything took both batteries, sliced the jib line and spray painted the freshly painted hull with figure eights in black.

I was afraid.

The potential buyer was none the wiser. He still came to see come see our sleek and beautiful boat. We had quickly scrounged up another battery, scrubbed the black paint off the side, and cited the weather as a reason not to take her out to sail so we would not have to address the fact that the jib could not be unfurled. The man said he loved the boat. We took him out for lunch and talked about life in the islands. The man drank our beer and laughed and waved some money around.

And then he disappeared.

My daughter is a speaker to the earth and a healer of energy. She lit a candle and wrote JACKAROO on a slip of paper and said a few positive words encouraging release and the manifestation of some cash in our pockets and the signing of transfer of title slips and she burned the paper.

It immediately turned into a black mass and burned for thirteen hours (interesting number, isn't it?). And when it finally went out, the glass holding the candle burst.

We believed the curse was broken.

And as of this writing, a young film-maker and his family are trying to get the cash together to offer our lovely mobile house on the water a new owner. Will the sale go through? Has Jackaroo's jilted heart mended?

We shall see.

PS,

The young film-maker bought the ship. He and his family moved into a little apartment in town and he got right to work scrubbing and painting and making Jackaroo his own.

Then one night, shortly after the purchase was completed, a storm swept through the region. Jackaroo's anchor dragged and she drifted helplessly across the bay.

Our young hero was beside himself and, lacking a dingy, plunged into the water and swam to Jackaroo side to save her. Of course, after boarding her, he realized he was powerless to remedy the situation. He was in need of another boat to pull her to safety. So he dove back into the black water and, in a panic, swam back to shore where he rounded up a Panamanian policeman. He frantically explained the situation and the policeman threw him in the back of the squad car, drove him to the center of town, and promptly dumped him out on a street corner and into the arms of a prostitute.

Hmmm, I think something was lost in translation.

To make a long story short, the young film-maker/new-boat-owner was able to snag a local fisherman complete with a fishing boat and the two of them rescued the drifting Jackaroo.

I am guessing that, given the profession of Jackaroo's new owner, there may one day be a box office hit titled something like, *Jackaroo and the Bocas Triangle,* or *The Black Night of Jackaroo,* or maybe *How to Go Crazy on a Ship.*

Either, I will pay extra for front row seats, or I will stay as far away from the movie theater as I can.

46. FACE ON THE CEILING

I do believe in the supernatural in all manner of things. I hear things occasionally that no one else hears—like my name being called, or the phone ringing so loud that it wakes me from a dead sleep but it isn't really ringing. But, I don't see much of anything. I listen to stories from people who do and I am always intrigued. I ask questions like, "Was it solid, or could you stick your hand through it?" And I listen carefully to the answers, somehow trying to validate the experiences, and at the same time figure out what is going on in some other, very close plane of existence.

So when we were living on Jackaroo, our 37ft sailboat with the lovely layout and the long, white leather couches, and the warm teak wood, and the green pillows thrown about, I often asked Lee to describe the people he saw ducking in and out of the companionway.

Of course, I never saw them.

He said they were usually short and often looked older and had dark complexions. Most were men and were as wrinkled as dried apricots.

Lee said he could see them clearly enough to see their clothing, which he usually described as rumpled looking. I think they must have been old sailors still wandering about wondering when we were going to sea.

I don't really like the idea of phantoms in my space. I never did.

I remember when my grandmother died. I had very real dreams of her ghost walking into my bedroom. I could not wake up. I was paralyzed from fear. It was like someone had stuffed rags in my mouth and I would struggle until finally the struggling broke the spell and I would wake up screaming.

This was not like that.

Often we slept on the long, white couches in favor of the soft bed in the stateroom because the stateroom was hot—sweat-running-down-the-middle-of-your-back hot—and we had air-conditioning in the main cabin.

The couches were on opposite sides of the boat. I slept on the starboard side and Lee on the port.

It was early or late, depending on how you count time—probably around 3:00 am—when I woke up. I lay quietly, gazing at the ceiling in the half-light from the moon. I was looking toward the ceiling over where Lee was sleeping, just sort of gazing into the middle space, not really looking at anything, when the face came into view.

It was huge.

It covered that entire side of the cabin. It had a big head, but no body. Kind of alien looking. There was no color. But, the details were clear and shifted in and out of view. It was very reptilian looking and just floated there on the ceiling.

Of course my first question was; *Did I do some kind of hallucinogenic drug right before I went to sleep?* To which, of course, the answer was, *No.* I was very curious about ayawaska, but had never had the opportunity to try the South American spirit drink and would probably be too afraid to drink it even if I was given the chance.

My second question was really a myriad of questions all rolled into one.

Was I dreaming? Why was I seeing an alien when I didn't believe in aliens? Was it really a demon? Was I having a problem with my eyes? Why was there no fear, or any feeling what-so-ever for that matter, attached to my viewing of the apparition, especially when I was so afraid of ghosts? Was I seeing something real that was in another dimension? Was it aware of my presence? It didn't seem to be. It was more like I could see it, but it couldn't see me.

It didn't move much, but it did seem to be speaking. It hovered there for the longest time, kind of turning this way and that a little, and giving me ample opportunity to explore it in detail.

I finally fell back to sleep with it still hovering there, just above Lee's sleeping form.

Talk about messing up your theology.

I have always been a Christian with your typical Christian beliefs. But, I have also studied my Bible extensively ever since the age of sixteen. I've read between the lines and done a ton of research trying to answer questions like; *Who were the Nephilim that were described as the offspring of fallen angels and earthly women?*

Maybe I was looking at one.

Maybe I was looking at something I'd never considered the existence of.

I have seen a few other things—lights mostly.

Lights are more easily dismissed than giant, hovering faces.

For now, I do not have any answers. So, I will file my experience in my mind until future light can be shed on the matter.

"Curiouser and curiouser," said Alice, as she explored the depths of wonderland...

47. ISLA SAN CRISTOBAL

There is a village on the island of San Cristobal that is peopled by Ngobe Bugle Indians. I do not know how long it has been there, but the houses seem fairly new, though weather beaten and full of holes. The people however, have lived on the island since before the days of Columbus.

We arrived in our panga after an uneventful bay crossing and a careful dodging of the reef. A long, well-built dock offered space to tie off the boat. Several kids greeted us. They were playing happily in the fetid water and did not ask us for anything (a rarity in these parts).

We had been in the village before, but wanted to walk the paths again. So, with our pockets filled with candy, we headed up the hill, past the swampy area where the first row of homes is built in the muck, and up onto the dry ground.

There was no road. Just a rough sidewalk hemmed in by banana trees. The homes were close together and children hung beneath the porches and chickens pecked the dirt for little bugs and dogs laid in the sun and flicked their tails at flies and old men smiled half-toothed smiles and cried, "Hola!" in cheery voices.

We handed out a few lollipops and swore the kids to secrecy, trying to keep the hoard of children we knew would find us when word got out at bay. Two little girls grabbed my hands and a boy walked with Lee. The boy looked up at Lee so often, I thought he was going to get a crick in

149

his neck.

It was hot and our bottled water supply was low, so we stopped at a little store with a walk-through window. In the window was a teenager who spoke a little English. He said they were out of water, but he had Coke. We bought one to share and asked if he knew where we could find the ladies who made the bags.

The Ngobe Bugle Indians are simple people who know how to live off the land. The know how to fish and collect food and medicine in the forest. And they are experts at weaving artful items from fibers that come from the pita plant, a plant related to the pineapple and bearing extremely long, thick leaves. After the leaves are harvested and dried, the Ngobe women separate the long leaf fibers. Then they roll them into thread and color the thread with natural dye from roots, flowers, and berries. The bags they weave from the thread can last up to thirty years and are strong enough to carry a heavy load of coconuts or cacao pods. This bag weaving is an art the Ngobe are well known for. But, with the advent of modern technology, the art is dying out.

I bought one of the bags, known locally as a mochilla, and was using it for my purse. I loved the all-natural look and thought maybe it was worth studying to see if we could market the bags back in The States. If we could give the Indians a good price for their artwork and sell a decent amount, it might encourage them to revive an age-old tradition. That would do two things. One: prevent the art from being lost to time. Two: provide an income for the families in transition between the old world and new—an income that made sense to them instead of forcing the women into Bocas Town to clean hotels or cook for almost nothing.

The boy behind the counter knew where the women were. The little girl who was holding my hand just happened to be the granddaughter of the president of the woman's art group. I didn't even know there was such a thing and was delighted to hear it. Could she bring us to see her grandmother? Of course!

We backtracked a few hundred yards to a wooden shack with a rustic sign boasting, *Art for Sale.* Apparently, I had missed it on the way up the hill. Word traveled so fast in the village that the little girl's grandmother beat us to the art shack and was already opening the door when we arrived.

Inside, beautiful handmade bags hung along the walls. Head-bands and belts hung there too. A table in the middle of the room was covered in red fabric to show off woven jewelry ornamented with seeds and shells.

We'd hit the jackpot.

I bought a bracelet the color of chocolate and cream and talked to Damiana, the president, about coming back to buy more of the bags. I needed the funds to do it and I wasn't sure where to find them. I wished I could have bought everything on the spot. I admit, I get frustrated with the time it takes to make things happen. Time is slow in the islands of Panama, like the clock is clogged with cacao paste and refuses to turn. But what frustrates me—the slowness of time—is also part of what makes the place so beautiful.

With my head full of ideas, I let Lee drag me back outside. We wandered through the village, handing out lollipops and talking to old men. We headed further up the hill to where the cacao trees grow and we caught the smell of fresh-baked bread. I love bread, especially when it's hot out of the oven. I had to track it down. Just off the path, several women were baking in a community oven. Well, *oven* is not really the right word. *Grill* is better. They were baking Jonny cakes, also known as coconut bread. A pan was set directly over the coals and covered to create a very effective oven that gave a lovely smoky flavor to the finished product. We bought two small, round loaves for twenty-five cents each and I started pulling at the warm bread immediately. The women were pleased with my reaction. It showed them how much I loved their bread!

A few minutes later, we were headed toward the end of the path, having passed a tied up pig (with whom we shared a little bread), a family of chickens (with baby chickens getting lost and found again), a couple kids (whom we also shared our bread), and an old man with only a few teeth left, but a very happy grin.

The soccer field was on the edge of town and it was gym-class time for the school kids.

Funny, now that I think of it, many kids were not in school. I know they have two sessions every day because they can't fit all the kids in at the same time. I think we were just seeing the younger kids out and about while the older kids were in class. But I also know, some of the kids simply cannot afford school. The classes are free to everyone, but the students are required to buy uniforms and all their own supplies. The cost is around five hundred dollars a year, just too much for some families.

Anyway, Lee could not help but get out onto the field with the kids, at least for a moment or two. The teacher laughed as he ran around trying to keep up with some very adept, albeit it young, soccer players.

It's what I love about living here. The connections we make. The teacher laughing, the kids out-playing the gringo, the women sharing their cooking skills, the boy at the grocery store helping us find the art-bag lady. This is community, very different from what I am used to back home. I like to call it an open society. In part simply because everybody is literally outside. It's hard to connect with people if you hide in your house all day.

Which brings me to the water-taxi guy and his family.

We saw him sitting on his porch with kids running everywhere. He spoke decent English. We recognized him from town. He had his own boat and used it to drive tourists from island to island. He worked six days a week, but stayed home on Sundays surrounded by his wife and children and grandchildren.

Lee asked him about a project he was working on in the front yard. It appeared to be a bathroom. A very simple one. But, it looked like the rain had washed away much of the work that was already done. The old man was happy to discuss his project and invited us in. Well, up. In fact, he insisted and let it be known in no uncertain terms that to refuse would be at the very least impolite if not downright rude. So we acquiesced.

A minute later, I was comfortably sitting in a rocking chair on the old man's porch. Lee was sitting in another rocking chair opposite me and the children were looking at us as if we were a friendly curiosity. One of the younger boys was actually tied to the porch, apparently so he would not fall off. Older kids came and went. The lady of the house was a broad shouldered woman wearing a long, black dress that nearly brushed the ground. She was a little less than five feet tall to my five foot six, so when I sat down and she stood up we were almost eye-level with each other. She noticed my mochila bag and my new bracelet and figured I would be a good candidate to see what she had created in her humble home. A moment later, I was presented with a parade of arts and crafts.

I chose a necklace made from seeds and shells. I put it on and she brought me a tiny mirror that looked like it had been taken out of an old jewelry box. I was happy with my treasure and paid her a wrinkled five-dollar bill.

Things took an interesting turn when the old man asked us if we wanted to rent his other house. I must admit, the idea brought up a lot of mixed feelings. The homes were very rudimentary. And none had bathrooms anything like what I was used to. No running water, no electricity, and very little, if any furniture. It would surely be an experience to remember.

Our host's house looked better than most. And it would be awesome to spend some time living in the village, right next door to the very people I wanted to help. It would be amazing to share their lives, to learn how to make coconut bread and help the old man finish his project and play with the kids in the afternoon.

Life can be challenging.

Desires battle each other.

Desire for an authentic experience. Desire for a shower—not just a hot shower, but any shower at all.

I will think about renting the old man's house.

In the meantime, I am happy I got to spend an afternoon hanging out with him and his family.

48. SPEAK LOVE

A dread-locked Rasta guy sat at the table next to me. Beyond him the calm water between the islands shimmered in the sun. Around him the bright colors of hand-crafted bird and fish mobiles, pineapple covered curtains, and red-checked tablecloths lent an air of reckless joy to the scene.

I started up a conversation with him. His English had that distinct Caribbean Creole flavor. I had no problem understanding him. I asked him if he understood me.

It was his answer that stuck with me for weeks to come.

Yes, he could understand me.

"I have a hard time understanding people when they speak fast," he explained.

"But I understand them good when they speak love."

49. CHRISTINE'S STORM

I have been in a lot of storms in my life. I have seen hurricanes and tornadoes and hail the size of golf balls and snow six feet deep. But I have never been so scared as I was that night.

We were living on our 60ft William Garden ketch. She was a beautiful old boat full of hand carved teak. We were anchored outside the marina on Isla Colon, Bocas Del Toro. It was a quiet bay where twenty-five ships or so were moored in a comfortable boating community. We made friends with other boaters and enjoyed the bond that living on the water can bring.

One evening, as the sun was going down, dark clouds gathered over the mountains on the mainland just a half-hour away.

"This one is going to be bad," Lee commented as we tightened lines holding tarps over the hatches.

I didn't think it looked different than any other on-coming storm and we didn't have any weather info saying it would be particularly bad. In fact, I thought it might even blow over and we would see nothing at all.

We left a few windows open in the main cabin in order to catch the breeze and I went below decks to cook dinner and relax with a glass of wine. I recall making homemade spaghetti from ripe tomatoes purchased at the market earlier that day.

We filled our teal colored wine glasses, lit a candle, and watched the sun fade into a cloudy night. A few drops of rain dampened the deck. Our panga, tied securely to the side of our sailboat, rested peacefully.

It was about ten o'clock when the wind started to pick up. It came from the mainland and across the bay. Normally storms came from the sea and we, protected by the island, didn't suffer the brunt of the waves and wind. This night was different. Rolling waves flung themselves toward shore, windswept and cresting. The panga began to buck like a young horse tied in its stall and ready to race. Lee went above deck to move the panga to the rear where it could have its head, but the winds were too strong to risk moving the little boat. I climbed the teak steps and peeked out into the night. The palms at the marina close by waved their arms in front of the bright marina light and cast frantic shadows across the shallows. Our mooring held. We had a safety anchor in case the line broke, but given the strength and direction of the wind, I was not convinced we'd be able to drop anchor and get it to catch before we hit shore if the unthinkable were to happen.

That was when Pretty came into view.

Pretty was the name of a 38ft sailboat anchored near us. She was a white sloop with wide, black stripes and was captained by a young Columbian who circumnavigated the world more than once. Often, when the winds changed direction and the boats all swung their bows into the breeze, we could see Pretty, floating there all pretty. But when she came into view on that stormy night, it was not with the changing of the wind, nor was she where she should be. She came careening toward us, her young captain at the helm trying desperately to steer her fiberglass hull away from us, her anchor dragging her sideways, like a bull in a china shop. We, on a fixed mooring and with no engine, were helpless to get out of her way.

Panama is below the hurricane belt and Bocas is considered a safe harbor for boats during the summer months. Crews from all over the world bring their ships to her calm waters. There are six marinas that I know of and you will find boats anchored in quiet coves by themselves or in small groups all throughout the thousand islands. I, like so many others, was under the false assumption that we would not be in any danger from storms. But wind is a funny thing. It does not need to be in the circular fashion of a hurricane to top eighty or ninety miles an hour. And though I do not know what the wind clocked that night, I did feel its merciless hand.

Pretty dragged by us, narrowly missing our bowsprit. She spun around, and for a few minutes, her anchor seemed to catch and hold. But it didn't last long. Soon she was fighting the gale again and this time she was not so lucky. She slammed into a nearby ship, doing considerable damage to both boats.

And she was not the only ship to be in trouble.

Walden was gone.

Walden was moored right next to us. Her mooring had broken a few weeks earlier and been replaced with new, stronger lines. But they didn't hold. I looked out into the night and there was no sign of her battered, white hull. I could not believe I had not seen her drift by. I must have been too captivated by Pretty's distress.

All told, ten sailboats went aground that night.

It was very close to the last night I spent on my boat.

I was badly shaken by the storm and gave up any thought of living on the water long term. Our William Garden was comfortable and roomy and, for a while, I had been under its spell. I dreamed of hosting friends and family on her spacious deck. But as a sailor friend once told me, "The sea doesn't care about you." She will have her way and we are forever at her mercy.

I will always love the sea. I have salt water in my veins. But that night, I decided I needed to get my feet on solid ground.

50. LA SOLUTION

There is a place in the bowels of Bocas Town that is wracked with stunning poverty. It has been dubbed, La Solution, which means The Solution. Although I cannot see how it is a solution to anything.

Ubaldino lived there.

Ubaldino was an orphan with a terrible skin condition. We first saw him walking the streets of Bocas Town, head hung down and arms wrapped around his frail body. He was twenty and had been an orphan for eight years. He and his brother, Aniwal, ten years the younger.

My story is not about Ubaldino. That story is too sad to tell.

My story is about his home in La Solution.

Thankfully, Ubaldino and his younger brother had been taken in by a kindly Ngobe Indian man. I really wanted to visit their home, but the first time I walked the paths of La Solution, I was not prepared for what I saw.

I followed the boys' caregiver down the streets of the poor part of town until he turned off the street and began walking down a path that ran into the marsh. Trash was strewn everywhere. Small clapboard homes with incomplete walls and curtains for doors stood on stilts to avoid inundation by the waters at high tide. The further we penetrated the marsh, the higher the stilts, and eventually we were walking above ground on wooden planks that wove together in a maze of partially rotting paths connecting the homes to each other.

I walked carefully, watching my step and really not wanting to fall into the refuse below. There were things in the bog that I didn't want to think about. There is no plumbing in La Solution...let's just leave it at that. Use your imagination!

When we got to what looked like the end of the road, or walkway, we entered the home of a gentle old woman. Ubaldino's home was accessible only by going through her house. Many of the floor boards in her home were rotten, and I took my time navigating across the living area to where the path continued on the other side of her home.

And then it got really hairy.

The wooden planks were nailed two-boards wide with the wall of another home pressed tight on one side and nothing at all on the other. The only way I could cross was arms wide open, basically trying to hug the wall because the path was so narrow. Several of the planks were not nailed down on one side or the other and they bowed as I walked across them. I was not entirely sure they would support me, but I was resolved to see our young friend's house.

Ubaldino's adopted papa reached out his hand to help guide me and finally I reached the door of his humble home.

The wood nailed together to form walls did not meet in many places and I could see out into the surrounding marsh. The wood also did not reach to roof in many places and cardboard filled in the gaps up high. Half of the living room did not even have a roof. That meant the rain came full inside. Downpours, rainforest typhoons in the living room.

There was no furniture but a few old milk crates turned upside down to sit on. There was a bed in Ubaldino's bedroom and it had a mattress on it that the two boys shared. However, there were no coverings for the mattress. No pillow, no blankets, no sheets. At night they wore as many clothes as they could to try and keep warm.

Yes, we did what we could to help. We bought zinc for the roof and bed clothes and food. Still, the experience overwhelmed me.

My life is changed. I cannot put into words the depth of what it has done to me. My view of the world has forever been transformed.

The most heartbreaking part of the whole thing was how a gentle, Indian man with absolutely nothing took in two orphan boys and offered them love, the most important thing!

51. UBALDINO

We lost a young man. His name was Ubaldino and he was twenty. He was an orphan who was deserted on the streets when he was about twelve with a two-year-old brother to care for. And he had a terrible skin disease.

It is so hard to understand why some are born into this world to undergo such suffering. Ubaldino could not work because of his condition. He believed he could never have a girlfriend. How heartbreaking—to believe you could never know that basic kind of love.

This is difficult for me. I cared for a young man that no one would hug because he looked like he has leprosy. Every time he saw me, he came running across the street open arms and yelling, "Mommy!" Sometimes I was frustrated with him because he wanted money to buy minutes for his cell phone and I knew he wasn't eating. But that is modern life. Children are children and they want their toys, even if it means giving up food to have them.

The problems in Bocas Del Toro, Panama are severe. They are difficult to solve. An orphan boy has nothing, but he wants to feel normal more than anything. Yes, he needs food. His belly is hungry. But more than that, he wants human interaction. He wants friends. He wants a family.

We will never be able to fix the world. But I hope that by reaching out to a young man and his little brother for a short time, maybe we brought some light into this place.

Rest in peace Ubaldino.

We love you.

52. LOLLIPOP GRAVE

We missed his funeral. We couldn't go because there was a storm. The kind where you might get lost at sea.

Heartbroken, a few days later we finally made it to the island where Ubaldino was laid to rest. The children met us at the dock. We asked them if they knew where Ubaldino was.

They did.

I thought an old man or a mama would bring us to his grave. I thought maybe my good friend Salsa would walk us there.

But Salsa was nowhere to be seen.

We bought lollipops for the kids.

Hand in hand they took us to the end of the village where the chocolate trees grow and the parrots squawk unceremoniously in the trees.

As we approached the graveyard, one little girl pointed out the spot where her baby sister was buried. So much sadness in such a beautiful place.

We found the mound of earth where our poor orphan boy was buried. We stood with the children in silence. We put the last lollipop on Ubaldino's grave.

Nothing else marked the pile of fresh soil.

The children understood. They each had their own lollipop and Ubaldino had is.

I wonder how long it will remain.

53. PICTURE THIS: POOR VILLAGE

You walk home from the store carrying two gallons of water, one in each hand. You turn off the main road and head down a dirt one where wooden houses built on stilts with curtains for doors sit back from the road and make room for half-dressed children to play. You pass the furniture builder working in his little shop and he waves at you and says, "Hola!" through the bandana wrapped around his face to prevent him from inhaling wood dust. A teenager rides by on a bicycle, his hat on backwards, and smiles at you. A momma rides by on a bicycle too. She steers around a puddle in the road and almost loses her balance as she tries to wave. You turn off the dirt road and onto a narrow sidewalk. You can see through the cracks in the walls of some of the brightly colored houses. Laundry is strung up everywhere because the day is sunny and the clothing will dry. A pitbull barks at you, practically scaring you out of your shoes. Three colorful chickens run by, crossing the sidewalk and ducking in under the leaves of a flowered bush. Two boys come running up behind you. They ask where the ball is. They want to play. You tell them to stop over later. They wave and keep running.

You open the chicken-wire fence that guards your house. You walk past the mango and banana trees and take a peek at your garden with the new row of tomatoes. You put the water jugs down, their handles have left imprints in your hands. You fumble for your keys and open the painted white gate that lets you into your enclosed porch—the one with the hammock. You pick up your water, walk across the porch, put the water down again, and fumble for more keys.

It's cool inside. Your home is built of cement. You open the windows and put your water on the counter just as the lady across the sidewalk calls out your name. You stick your head back outside and answer her kindly.

"You want I give you some of the limes from my finca?" she asks in her thick Creole English.

You are blessed. She thinks of you often.

"Oh, I would love some!" you answer.

You leave your water to wait and go meet your sixty-something-year-old neighbor at the fence.

She hands you the limes and confides in you. "I saw someone come and knock to your door," she says. "I think he was wanting to cut your yard. I told him you were no home and to come back some nother time."

You thank her for looking out for you. She has taken you under her wing. She knows this territory and she says now you are family.

You listen as she tells you about her day. She had a call from her sister and her niece came to visit and help with the wash. She has an appointment to see the shoulder doctor in the city next week. She is sure he will fix her aching arthritis. You picture her carrying heavy loads up the stairs and into her wooden house. You remember her scrubbing her painted walls and pruning her trees and you wonder how a woman of her age has so much energy.

You cannot imagine she really needs to go see a doctor. You think it is just the modern technology that draws her. In spite of her deep understanding of culture and self-sufficiency, she seems enthralled at the new gizmos and gadgets she sees on TV.

She finishes her story and apologizes for molesting you. You love the word. It's the Spanish word they use that means *to bother*.

You assure her it's no bother and you tell her you have two star apples that look like they will be ripe tomorrow. You promise to give her one and she smiles.

The water still sits on the shelf, forgotten.

Life in a poor village is so rich.

54. WARTS AND CHOCOLATE

I saw him today. A little boy whose face was dirty and clothes were dirty and hands and feet were dirty. He was a little shy when he approached me. His thick Spanish was too hard for me to understand and my Spanish is getting pretty good. Then again, he was a little Indian boy, so maybe he wasn't speaking Spanish at all. But he definitely was asking for something.

His eyes were big and brown and warts covered his little hands.

I don't know where he came from. Most of the children here in Panama don't wander the streets. Most of the kids are clean and happy. They walk nicely with their parents in town and have clean faces. I looked around to see if I could see his family, but all I saw was a nicely dressed Indian family watching the scene unfold while they waited for a taxi. There was no one else on the street.

Lee pulled out a dollar and handed it to the boy. "Here," he said. "Go get something to eat."

The boy took the dollar in his little wart-covered hands and ran into the foul smelling grocery store. I looked inside after him to see if I could spot an adult who might belong to this urchin.

Nothing.

The Chino behind the counter (that is what they call them here—the

Chinese who own all the grocery stores in town) took the dollar and handed the boy a piece of chocolate wrapped in gold foil and handed him some change.

A moment later the boy was in the street again, this time with a half-opened piece of gold foil in his hands and chocolate in his teeth. That and a big smile on his dirty face.

In all honesty, I don't know if the boy was hungry. I couldn't understand what he asked of me. And I don't know if he has a family. Just because I didn't see them doesn't mean they weren't close by. But I do know this. He loved the candy.

55. PAULY-SIGHT

Pauly was blind. Every day he sat on a plastic chair next to the dock at the two-stall boathouse on a calm oxbow in the Almirante River. He watched our panga. Lee called out to him when we arrived to take our panga out for the day, "Hey Pauly, its Gringo!" Pauly smiled, his teeth still blazing white in his old black face. "How you doing today?" Lee would ask and we would banter a bit about the weather and Pauly would unlock the door to the boathouse, walk barefoot down the clean wood planks, and grab a long stick to open up the outside doors so we could leave the safety of the boathouse for the still river and, possibly, the salty bay.

One day I saw Pauly riding his bicycle. (Yes, blind Pauly rode a bicycle. I have no idea how he did it!) He'd left his post for a jaunt across town—to gather supplies I might guess, perhaps rice and bananas, some chicken, and maybe a bottle of Coke. Lee hollered when he rode by, "Hey Pauly, its Gringo!"

Pauly smiled.

The day our sailboat—anchored out in the salty bay—was broken into, we told Pauly our story as he let us back in the boathouse. "Maybe they wanted to molest you," he offered. I like how they use the word *molest* here to mean bother. I felt like I'd been molested. We told Pauly the thief didn't steal anything. He just broken into the boat and dragged things out of cupboards and left a mess. We told him that this was the third time our 37ft ketch had been broken into in almost as many days.

"Indians," some said.

"They trying to thief you," others said

But Pauly thought maybe it was something darker, something less innocent. Take my blanket and I will be upset that you violated my space, but I will remind myself that maybe you simply needed to be warm.

Take my fishing pole and I will be frustrated that I only got to use it once, but I will count myself lucky that, should I desire, I can by a new one and maybe you need it to feed your family.

But break into my sail-wearing home on the water and take nothing, and I will be afraid.

Maybe you are targeting my boat specifically. Maybe you are looking for something you can't find. Maybe my boat, bought in an old pirate town in the remote islands of the Caribbean, has a history I know nothing about. Maybe you are entangled in its story and are up to no good. And maybe I will be caught in the crossfire.

Pauly may not have been able to see with his watery red-rimmed, dark eyes. But I fear his second site was better than mine.

And I still don't have the answer as to who broke in to my boat.

Or why.

56. SLEEPING SNAKES

We met Anthony, Rodolfo Anthony, on a walk out of town and up the hill that overlooks the islands. He called us into his yard after explaining to us about the very dangerous sleeping snakes that live in the area. He said they love to sleep all curled up and if you walk by too loud and wake them ooo..., they will chase you and bite you and you will die. But if you carry a machete and use it to poke at the grass and the ground in front of you, the snakes will know the sound of the machete and will run away. He said they are very smart and he didn't know but he figured God made them that way.

We vowed to always carry a machete when walking in the grass and then we followed him into his yard (minus a machete).

Anthony told us he is descended from Jamaica. He told us all about his grandparents and how they taught him a lot of things about how to live. Things that came from the old country. He gave us the tour of his garden. (A term I use loosely as it was really just what appeared to be a tangle of weeds.) He showed us some leaves that smelled faintly of mint and are good for tea and he showed us some leaves that didn't smell like much of anything but come from a plant with a tiny purple flower and are good to get rid of colds. He wanted to show us his okra, but a big wind had blown the plant down and broken its root. He lamented a little over it, but then went on to show us sugar cane and guaba—a pod containing seeds covered in what looks like natural marshmallow.

I loved Anthony. He was tall and wiry and probably about sixty, but with the body of an athlete. His skin was dark, but not as dark as some, and his hair held just a little bit of grey.

He talked of red frogs and green frogs and yellow frogs and he talked of how the giant locusts must contain a poison because nothing eats them.

He showed us a red fruit that looked just like a water apple, but wasn't, which is a very important fact because, he explained, "THIS fruit is extremely poisonous before it is ripe. They use it cook and I will not cook my catfish without it. But it cannot be eaten until it is ripe and it splits apart and releases a toxic gas."

"Everything has a time," he said. "And we must wait until the time is ready."

I felt as if I were learning from a very wise guru who was using nature to explain the truth of life to me.

We thanked Anthony for his garden tour and his wonderful hospitality and as we were getting ready to say good bye, he stopped us and introduced his family. His wife waved out the window of their wooden home that stood up high on stilts. His grandchildren were peeking out the door next door. His daughter was sitting in a little chair just inside the house, her beautiful black hair tied up on top of her head.

"Just a minute," he said and he walked through the fence next door, scooped up his peeking grandchildren, and brought them out to us. A four-year-old girl with long black ringlets and blue ribbons in her hair and a seven-year-old boy who had skipped school and stayed home because of the rain.

"My babies," he said.

The joy on his face was contagious.

We thanked Anthony over and over for his time and his knowledge and for the bag of ripe naranjiots he'd given us to bring home.

174

"Come back and I will take you up the hill to see the view of the islands. Bring your friends and I will show you all this area and everything I know."

"We will come back," we promised. "And we will bring our friends!"

57. WRECKED

You know, living in someone else's house does not mean you understand their way of living.

I went to Central America with a carry-on suit case and a back-pack and I never looked back. I lived all through Mexico and Costa Rica and I ended up in Panama where I rented a little house in a very poor neighborhood. Why? Why live in a poor neighborhood? Why on earth would someone want to struggle with getting running water and know that hot water was simply never going to be available? Why would someone who had a comfortable home in the US choose to hang their laundry out in a country where it never stops raining and things mold before they ever get dry? Why would someone choose to live where the neighbor's house is built in such a fashion that the wood slats are not lined up close enough to each other to keep you from looking right outside? The mud is red. The neighbors do their wash in a bucket and cook over an open fire. There is no road, only a narrow sidewalk.

The place is poor.

The other day, I met a local in town and told him I lived in Almirante. He looked at me surprised and with barely veiled distain remarked that I must live in the nice part of town. When I told him I lived in Colondrina, he smiled wide and embraced me in a bear hug and exclaimed, "My people!"

That is why.

I live here because I want to feel what they feel. I want to be immersed in their culture on a day to day basis. I want to know their names and the names of their children. I want to stop by and chat and bring my star apples over and have them give me their limes. I want to congratulate them on the birth of their babies and mourn the loss of their loved ones. I want to understand them from the inside.

But it is impossible to do that.

I am from a different culture. My memories are full of different things. My education and travel and life experience has filled my head with what makes me, me. And their life experience is very different than mine.

I will never know what it feels like to know nothing different than this small town and its people. And in all honesty, I am not sure I will ever be as simply happy as they are. It is still a mystery to me. King Solomon who was famous for being so wise said, "With much knowledge comes much sorrow." I believe he was correct. I see what looks like the pain these people deal with every day. But on their faces, I see smiles. They are genuinely happy. Yes, they mourn and they mourn deeply, but they understand that it is part of life and they allow it to come and then they move past it. They love deeply. They are surrounded by family and that, to them is everything. They wake up in the morning to the chickens and the sun and when it rains, instead of complaining that the weather is bad, they are thankful for the water it provides so they can do their laundry.

Oh, my heart is wrecked.

I came to embrace the challenge of a poor community in a third-world country and it kicked my butt. Not because I couldn't handle the hardships, but because I was unprepared for the beauty.

58. NOTES ON POVERTY

I have lived in Central America for five years. I lived without hot water for well over a year and without refrigeration for nine months. I lived without electricity for two months and with very limited electricity for another seven. I lived without running water for three months. I collected and used rain water for all my household needs for eighteen months. I lived in the rain forest without a dryer for three years and without a washer for two years. I washed my clothing by hand in salt water for seven months.

Why am I telling you all this?

It wasn't really intentional. It just happened to be the way things worked out. But I am glad they worked out that way. It gave me the opportunity to better understand what I need and what I don't need. I found it is actually pretty easy to live without refrigeration as long as you don't eat a lot of meat. Of course I had to give up ice cream and go really short on cheese, butter, yogurt, and other dairy products. But it felt good knowing that I was not dependent on a fridge. It felt good knowing that if the power went out it just meant I wouldn't have lights that evening. It felt good being able to wash my clothes by hand and hang them out to dry. It was a lot of work, I admit. And I am so very thankful for modern conveniences when I do have them, especially hot water!

I lived in a lot of places during my time in Central America, but of my favorite place is where I live now. It's a poor community on the mainland in Bocas Del Toro, Panama. I live across the street, no across the sidewalk—there is no street—from a Jamaican lady named Noile. She is sweet as can be and brings me fruit from her trees and gets me out of trouble with the locals when they think it's OK to take advantage of me.

The lady next door is Ngobe Bugle, full blooded. She has a gaggle of children, I am not sure how many, but the two-year-old's name is Calel which is Superman's Cryptonian name. Her husband came over once to ask to borrow five dollars for food for the baby. Her oldest child came over another time to ask the same thing. I loaned them the money and they paid me back, a rarity in these parts.

There is something wonderful about living in a poor community. The kids help me with my garden. Lee plays football with them in the yard. I am becoming part of the community and getting to see what it's like from the inside.

And I have learned a lot.

So what have a learned about poverty?

1. It isn't what we think it is.

2. It seems to stem from money.

Interesting story...

I went to visit the Watsi in Costa Rica. They live in the foothills of the Talamanca Mountains near the Caribbean coast. My visit was very enlightening to say the least.

I went with a friend of mine and a guide. We were dropped off by the taxi at the entrance to a path through the woods where chocolate trees and mango trees vied for space in the thick jungle. A blue morpho butterfly, a sign off good luck according to the Mayans, flitted across the path and I watched his blazing blue wings catch the light as he disappeared between the trees. Ahead was a bridge, a swinging bridge.

Now there are swinging bridges built for adventures seekers that want to see the beauty of Costa Rica, and then there are swinging bridges that are built for everyday use by local people. The two are not the same. Trust me, the adventure seeker's bridges are much safer.

This particular swinging bridge was strung between the two steep sides of a ravine. Beneath it was a rushing river. We climbed up about oh, twenty steps to get to the bridge. The ravine plunged four stories down. But I wasn't looking.

I love adventure. In fact, I seek it out. But when I encounter real experiences, not the Disneyland kind, I have learned to take them seriously and be careful. The bridge did swing quite a bit and we crossed it one at a time to avoid weird cross-swinging. The railings were quite low making it difficult to balance correctly because you had to lean quite far forward to grasp the cable safety lines. I imagine this was because the Watsi are small people. The bridge was built for them, after all, not for silly tourists like me.

But the worst part was the condition of the wooden slats. It always comes back to those rotting wooden slats. Some were not nailed down properly. Some were showing signs of wear and some had actual holes in them.

I chose my steps carefully, wondering how much of an idiot I was as the fall would not exactly be fun. But I was determined to act as if it didn't bother me in the least and I really was excited about visiting those gentle people.

On the other side, I thankfully put my feet on green earth again. The village was charming. The grass was trimmed, probably with a machete, but possibly with a weed-whacker. The homes were built on waist-high stilts, I imagine to keep everything dry and to keep unwelcomed wild-type visitors from making uninvited visits. I know snakes are a real problem in Coast Rica and fer-de-Lance and bushmaster both live in the area. BIG black panthers also populate the surrounding jungle. Not that a little high-rise would keep these creatures completely at bay, but they might discourage home invasion a bit.

The roofs were of woven palm leaves, beautifully done in a straight overlapping line pattern. The walls were wood and only went up half way, allowing the breeze to blow through the homes and giving a feeling of real connectedness with the vine covered trees that stretched so far overhead you had to put a crick in your neck to see the tops.

The village owned a sacred grove of cacao trees that were guarded by hand-carved stone statues of warriors with red painted eyes, most likely dyed red with achiote berries. And I also noticed a hand-carved crocodile on the path to the cacao trees, another totem designed for protection and possibly good luck.

The people of Watsi have been at that particular location for five generations. The oldest resident and original founder of the village just died two years ago at the ripe old age of one hundred and twelve! I got to meet his great grand-daughter and I also got to meet the village medicine man. Both spoke fluent Spanish and their native tongue. My Spanish isn't great, but it is tolerable and I was excited to chat a little with them.

They have made some changes over the years and adopted a few western things, most importantly, western clothes. The young lady showed me an example of a man's loin cloth/skirt made from bark pulled into tiny threads and woven into a stiff cloth. I said it didn't look very comfortable. She agreed. She was wearing a green skirt and white top and the medicine man was wearing a white t-shirt and jeans and had several strands of beautiful stones and teeth hanging about his neck. There were a few plastic storage containers in the room, but other than that, everything appeared to be basically the same as it would have been when the village was founded.

It was clean.

Other village members were working in a happy and industrial fashion. Smoke was coming from the open fire in the kitchen and lunch smelled delicious. Kids were laughing and playing. A few dogs were lolling about, healthy looking dogs, I might add, not the typical rib revealing pups of other Indian villages I had been in.

As I listened to their story, I learned that about ten years ago, the government allocated money to build modern homes in the Watsi village. They purchased concrete and glass and rebar and all the building materials needed for modern houses and were ready to make what they considered to be a generous donation to these simple people. But when the elders of the village got wind of it, they wanted nothing to do with it.

Never-the-less, the government insisted that they had already bought the materials and they were going to drop them off and the villagers could do whatever they wanted to with the stuff.

So, a few months later men came across that same bridge I so carefully walked across carrying loads of heavy modern building materials and they unceremoniously dumped everything in the lower part of the village.

And there it sat.

The older people in the village did not touch it, but eventually, one by one, younger people started building houses.

Now there is a section of the Watsi village the consists of small, modern concrete homes.

I went there to observe and take some photos.

I was disappointed.

The concrete homes are not well cared for like the traditional grass-roofed homes. The area is dirty. It has that distinct look of poverty seeping in.

I don't know why. I don't know if it is because the homes are owned by people in the younger generation and they just don't keep things nice like their grandparents do or if it is because they don't know how to take care of these kinds of homes. But I do see that the traditional, thatched-roof and bamboo homes are lovely and the concrete ones are rapidly falling into disrepair.

Which brings me to the conditions of another village I have been in.

There is a Ngobe village on the far end on Isla Colon, the main island in Bocas Del Toro, Panama. It is Ubaldinos' La Solution. I don't know why they call it that because it certainly is not a solution to anything. It is built in the marsh. The homes are on stilts above the water and wooden walkways run from house to house to provide a dry place to walk. Of course the wood is rotting in many places and not nailed together in some and bowed in others and altogether dangerous to walk on. And believe me, you would not want to fall into the marsh.

Trash comes in with the tide. Tons of it. But that is not the worst problem. The homes do not have indoor plumbing. What should go into a septic tank goes directly into the water below the houses. And during low tide, the kids play in it.

Waterborne disease is a big problem and birth defects are rampant.

But everyone has a cell phone.

These people want to transition into a more modern life. They want to connect with friends and family and a cell phone gives them the power to do that. They are very relational people. Family means everything to them. They like to wear nice clothes. Most of the women have jewelry and purses and the kids are dressed in nice clothing. The men usually wear jeans and button up shirts and the women are almost always found in skirts. The school kids' white shirts are spotless, which I have no idea how they do, because I can't keep my white shirts clean to save my life. But the health conditions are deplorable.

Most of the people who live in La Solution are from another island further out called San Cristobal. San Cristobal has no roads and just a few sidewalks. It is MUCH cleaner and has plenty of land with big fincas, or farms, owned by the Ngobe. So I asked people who live in La Solution why they live there and not on San Cristobal where they are from. Most are there because they want to live closer to town so they can find work.

Which brings me back to the money issue.

These people could be living on a farm, raising chickens and growing their own food and building homes from bamboo and palm, but they feel the need to modernize. They want to live in town. They say they want to work, but the reality is, most of them do not. And THAT is what is creating the conditions they are living in.

Then there is the rice and sugar issue.

Rice fills your belly. Sugar makes things taste good. But together they do not provide the nutrition needed for healthy development and growth.

The Ngobe who live in the Bocas Del Toro region of Panama are traditionally fishermen and farmers. They have been living off the land since Christopher Columbus landed there and tried to steal it from them. In an effort to integrate into modern society, they have started selling the food they produce. Which seems like a good idea. But here's how it goes.

A fisherman catches a fish and bring it to market. He doesn't eat the fish, because it brings a good price. So he sells it for a few dollars then takes the money and buys sugar and rice (the government gives the Ngobe special prices on these items and they typically buy them in fifty pound bags). Then he takes the rest of the money and buys minutes for his cell phone (and possibly beer).

It seems like a good trade off on the surface. But let's expand it.

He sells his fish. The he goes into the jungle and collects super fruits like mammon chino (what we call lychee) and wild limes and coconuts and bananas and rose apples and wild mangoes and papaya and bread fruit and jack fruit...should I keep going? The point is, the jungle is packed with amazing, super nutritious, delicious fruit. So he goes and collects it and brings it to market.

He does not eat it.

Remember, all he eats is rice and sugar. And all he feeds his children is rice and sugar. Yes, rice fills a hungry belly and sugar tastes good, but it is not enough. Your brain needs good fats to develop properly, the kind that fisherman would have found in his fish. And it needs protein and vitamins and minerals. And those kids need the nutrition in order to learn properly. In fact, I believe the overall IQ of these people is dropping due to their lack of good nutrition, which they have, but they sell, because they want minutes for their cell phones.

So there is the problem.

I have been all over the world and I see that the younger generation desires to move into a modern world. One they see on TV and on the internet. I understand the desire to stay in touch with loved ones and I also see what the love of money is doing to entire people groups. I would like to re-define poverty and I will do just that in a subsequent chapter. But for now let's just be aware of the problems caused by the pursuit of wealth and modern amenities.

Some solutions could possibly be:

1. The Ngobe have a simple art form they have been practicing for centuries and I believe we could market that and bring money in by selling art instead of selling food.

2. Teach gardening to the children. They love to dig in the dirt and just about anything will grow in the area. We could dramatically increase the amount of food production by making gardening cool again.

I know there are lots of other ideas out there, and I am sure you will think of some. I would love to hear them. Right now, these two seem fairly easy to do and sustainable, which is very important. We can't teach gardening by buying lots of seeds and miracle grow. We have to teach them how to use the seeds from food they eat and how to garden organically with whatever is available locally for zero cost.

But it's the making these things cool that is the really important part.

The younger generation is all about what is happening on the TV and the internet. They look at what the first world countries are doing and try to emulate that. Oddly enough, here in the US there is a big movement to go back to organic gardening and self-sustaining lifestyles.

So what if we could connect the two? What if we could bring people in first world countries to third world countries where they could participate in a vibrant exchange of education and culture? What if we first worlders could learn about living with rain water and solar power and harvesting wild food and medicine and we could teach third worlders modern gardening methods and how to harvest plants without damaging them long term and how to fish sustainably.

It all sounds great, doesn't it?

I think we could make some progress starting with one small community and getting to know the people and building trust and working together. It would take dedication and time. We could put together a program where first worlders could come visit and work and share and inspire and be inspired...well I am getting ahead of myself, but this is my idea and it is in the works.

Baby steps. We will take baby steps, but at least we will start.

59. NOTES ON THE HOMELESS

First I want to qualify this by making sure you understand I am writing about my experience and that involves the homeless in Central America which, I am sure is different than the homeless in the US. It seems to me that there are more homeless people in the US than in the areas I lived and visited, which seems odd. And I will address what I think may be a reason for that in my Notes on Re-defining poverty.

For now, I want to talk about Jerry and Eddy and Good Times and oh, the guy sleeping in the flies....

I like these guys. They have cool stories to tell and they generally are very nice and even respectful. Once they learn you are not going to give them money, that is.

Giving money to those in need can be a problem. It seems like the right thing to do when someone who doesn't smell very good and is dirty comes up to you with tears in their eyes, rubbing their tummy and making the universal motion for *give me something to eat*. Sometimes it is the right thing to do. But not always.

This is a lesson I had to learn the hard way.

In many third world countries begging is seen as completely acceptable because "those gringos have a lot of money and we poor people don't and therefore they should give us money." I have been approached by many people asking for a handout and I always used to give it. Then there was the day I was sitting in the park and had no cash on me and no cash coming in for a few days and I was going to need to go back on the banana-coconut diet, which I have been on before. The banana-coconut diet is the diet you go on when you have no money at all and you need to eat food that is basically free. Bananas go for five cents apiece and coconuts can easily be found along the beaches. You just need a machete to get into them so you can drink the life giving coconut water and scoop out the nutrient packed coconut meat. It isn't a bad diet, short term that is.

Anyway, I was preparing myself for a few days of this particularly nutritious diet when along came a guy begging for a dollar. I really wasn't in the mood. I had been living in Central America for four years and I could tell the difference between a guy who really needed the money and one who was either too lazy to work or was going to use it to buy drugs. Side note: cocaine is cheaper than marijuana in Bocas Del Toro.

Well he was very insistent, rude in fact. So I took out my LAST dollar and held it up to him and in butchered Spanish I told him, "This is my last dollar. I need it to buy some soup and then I will have no money. If I give it to you, I will not get any soup." And he reached out and grabbed it out of my hand!

ARRRG! (Pirate talk for ARE YOU SERIOUS!)

In truth, that was the worst episode I had of homeless bullying. And I don't think he was really homeless.

In other cases, I have given money one day and been accosted the next for more, usually a greater amount and often with an, "I deserve it. You better give it to me," attitude. It can get a little uncomfortable. You want to give at first, and then after getting taken so many times, you don't want to give at all. But I don't think either answer is right. Of course sometimes there are situations where the person really is hungry and it is appropriate to give. But that isn't really what I am talking about here.

What I have discovered is the power of NO.

After all, if you give a man a fish, he will eat for a day and if you teach a man to fish, he will go broke buying fishing gear...I mean he will eat for a lifetime, right?

That is sort of the principle here.

I learned how to say, "No," firmly and politely. But then I didn't just walk away. I didn't tell the guy I figured he was going to use my money to buy drugs (even if I figured he was going to) and I didn't tell him that I didn't have any money (because he KNEW I did, even if I didn't). Instead, I told him *no* and then I changed the subject.

I asked him how he was doing. I asked him about his family. I asked where he grew up and if he had brothers and sisters. I asked what he liked to do and what his aspirations were. (I didn't use that word though).

And that's when things started to change.

The guys living on the street are there for a reason. And giving them a handout doesn't not fix it. But getting to know them gives them something they really need. It gives them simple human connection.

Let me tell you about Good Times. His real name is Sergio but we call him Good Times because he likes to hand out the local free newspaper called The Good Times in return for tips. He can be very annoying. Every time you walk by, he tries to sell you a free paper. But that isn't the worst of it. He goes on and on about everything in the paper and expects you to listen like a good student and nod your head in agreement with everything he says.

The first time I met Good Times, I bought his paper and listened to his spiel. The second time, I ditched him and tried not to make eye contact.

But then, as I got braver, I got to know him. I told him I did not want a paper and I told him (the harder part) that I did not need to hear about everything in the paper. Instead, I asked him about himself.

Good Times sleeps in the park because his mother married a guy who doesn't like him and will not let him in the house even though it is on the street corner right next to the park. The guy his mother married is not a nice guy. I know. I've met him.

Good Times is in his thirties and you might think, well he is plenty old enough to get a home of his own. But that is not how things work in Central America. Families stick together and often many generations live in the same house so they can support each other. Good Times is a very smart guy, but he is not very savvy. He can read and do research, but he has trouble finding a job in town. He is rather obsessive about his paper and can't seem to function well in, say a carpentry position. Jobs are extremely limited on the island and poor Sergio just doesn't have the skills that are in demand.

One evening I was out late and heartbroken from an argument I'd had with a loved one. I bought myself a plate of chicken and rice and sat on a park bench. Along came Good Times with every intention of selling me a free newspaper. But when he saw I was in distress, he folded his newspaper, put it in his bag, and sat down on the bench beside me. Then he pulled a to-go plate of fish and rice out of his bag and offered me some of his food.

We shared dinner that night, Good Times and I. I gave him some of my chicken and he gave me some of his fish and we both fed the street dog sitting at our feet. Good Times told me I could sleep on the bench next to his and I would not need to be afraid all night because he would look out for me.

A few months later I saw Good Times out late in the evening again. His mother died. Tears streamed down his face. He was hungry. And now there was no chance of him going home to the house of his dead mother and his ugly step-father. I bought him some fried chicken and rice and I hugged his neck.

I would like to get Sergio off the street, but I can't. At least not right now. It is a comfort to me that he is eating most days and Bocas is warm, so he is not in danger of freezing. As I build my friendship with Sergio, I hope a good solution will come to me. I am trying to find a sustainable way to help him fit in.

Just like Eddy.

Eddy is a drug dealer. He calls me Boss. No, I am not his supplier. Eddy calls me Boss because after he begged me for money several times and I told him *no,* I got to know Eddy. He doesn't want to be a drug dealer. It's risky and it isn't very profitable. (Believe it or not.) Eddy just wants to make pinchos and sell them in the street. Pinchos are fried meat on a stick, usually served with a spicy sauce and a tortilla. All Eddy needs is a small food cart. He has done the research and has found a reasonable way to make a food cart for much less money than it would cost to buy one. So instead of giving Eddy a few bucks and wondering what he is doing with it, I am trying to raise money to help Eddy build his food cart. Then maybe I can give him some simple tutoring in how to run a small business. Then there would be a valid reason for him to call me Boss.

You get it.

Jerry told me the most exciting story about being dedicated to Satan at birth, studying magic for three years so he would be prepared to go into the drug trade, being killed over a hundred times, having secret knowledge about the location of the hole in the sea where the gold is and his spiritual not-very-nice guide The Engine. It all sounds crazy, but, given the circumstances, I believe the stories are real. Jerry has been through the ringer. He pushes a shopping cart around town, sleeps on the beach, bathes in the sea, and loves to clean. He carries a broom, a dustpan, and a rake in his shopping cart and he keeps the park spotless, free of charge. Jerry will accept a free cup of coffee, but he doesn't want you feed him. He makes creamed corn-flour mixed with water in a coffee pot that he plugs into an outlet in the park. I have cooked Raman noodles in a coffee pot. It works great! I hope to get Jerry a job working for the town. He already cleans the park. It would be great if he could get paid for it.

The point is, it takes getting to know these guys to start coming up with real solutions. It is so easy to hand out a dollar, or to just walk past and do nothing because you assume they will use that dollar to buy beer. (They probably will.) But it isn't the buying beer that is a problem. WHY are they buying beer? The answer to that question is where the problem lies.

Which brings me to the guy sleeping in the swarm of flies.

I was in Costa Rica on a solo trip and staying in a tiny town on the Caribbean called Chauita. It has a lovely state park complete with sloths and monkeys, beautiful beaches, and adorable little crafty shops and restaurants. It was late afternoon and I felt impressed to go down to the local pub and have a beer. Yes, I felt impressed to do this. So off I went.

I had just been online expressing my heart felt agreement with the idea that people need to be loved out of drug addiction. In fact, in a moment of passion, I threw my heart at God and said, "Please, let me do this!"

Anybody ever here the phrase, "Be careful what you wish for"?

So I sat and had a local beer and listened to some wonderful live Calypso music and when my one beer was gone, I felt impressed to get up and leave. So I did.

I walked across the street to the park and was stopped almost immediately by a swarm of flies coming from a park bench. I walked over to see what was going on and a man was lying there face down, passed out I assumed, and literally covered in hundreds of flies.

At first I wondered if he was alive. His body posture seemed like he was sleeping, so I asked a street guy close by what the problem was. The guy who answered me was short and small and mostly likely Bribri Indian. His hair was dark and he was fairly grimy. Let's call him Bribri Guy for lack of a better name. So Bribri Guy explained that Fly Guy had...and he gave me a single word in Spanish. (Of course his whole conversation happened in Spanish.) I had no idea what the word meant, nor can I recall it now. So Bribri Guy explained that it was when a guy loses his wife and then drinks until he loses his job and his house and ends up on a park bench passed out with urine all over himself and flies swarming him. I didn't know they had a word for such a thing, but it must happen fairly often so I guess they had to coin a phrase for it.

About that time Fly Guy rolled over and sat up. He pants were wet. Snot dripped from his nose. His nice button up shirt looked like it had been slept in for several days. His dark hair was rumpled. He looked like he had been beaten up and blood was freshly dried on several parts of him. And, when he saw that I was asking about him, he immediately started sobbing.

I carefully selected a spot to sit on the concrete bench where there didn't appear to be any blood or other bodily fluids. It was a little farther away from him than I normally would have sat because he pretty much destroyed every part of the bench. I asked him why he was crying.

"Because Jesus will never forgive me!" he wailed and went back to sobbing.

Oh my...I had just begged God to send me to someone who needed to be healed from addiction by love. My heart broke and though I wanted to hug this poor man, I consciously recoiled from him. I asked him to tell me his story and he told me about how his wife, whom he adored, left him. He told me how much he missed her and how she would not come back to him. He told me Jesus would never forgive him for that and he cried.

He was quite drunk and, seeing a food cart nearby and thinking a little something in his stomach might make him feel better and help him shake off the alcohol, I offered to buy him something to eat. But he didn't want anything. So I asked him what he did want and his response was exactly what I knew it would be, "a hug."

This is the point when you look at yourself full in your private mirror and you make a decision to push past your comfort zone. You acknowledge how you are feeling inside, the contradiction of it, the compassion and revulsion, and you jump in. You throw caution to the wind and you hug whole heartedly and let someone snot on you. Once you break the barrier, it is broken. From that point on, in that particular situation, it seems you can do anything.

I hugged him and I comforted him and I laid my hand on his shoulder and prayed for him. And when I did, he immediately looked up at me and smiled. He FELT the love of God go through him. It instantly gave him relief. He shared with me how both his brother and sister committed suicide. He told me he had felt like he did not want to live.

I know I cannot make people's choices for them and I know I am not responsible for this man. But in that moment, it is hard not to feel the weight of responsibility. I am thankful I saw him there that day covered in flies. I am thankful I was able to get out of myself enough to reach out to him.

I did buy him something to eat eventually, and as he sat there and talked and ate, he seemed to come to himself a little more. I assured him that Jesus still loved him and that of course Jesus would forgive him. I wished I could take away his pain. When I got up to leave him Bribri Guy came over and asked me for money. I refused. He was angry. I didn't give in.

It can be really difficult sometimes, knowing when to give and when not to. The trick is in getting outside yourself to give the really important thing, which is usually your time or a hug.

I saw Fly Guy the next morning. He was still wearing the same clothing, but he looked much better.

I do wish I had a better name for him. How about Forgiven Guy?

60. RE-DEFINING POVERTY

Poverty = Lack of Money.

Ok so let's start with this. If poverty is the lack of money, and that is generally how we think of it, then who is in poverty?

A. A person with a lovely $300,000 house with a mortgage of $250,000 and a nice new car worth $20,000 with an $18,000 loan.

B. A person with a $30,000 simple house with no mortgage and a bicycle.

If you do the simple math you see that the guy with the debt is obviously the poor one. Now you can come up with all kinds of reasons why he really isn't in poverty. But let's look a little deeper.

In Central America there are no loans. Yes, you can get a gringo loan from a non-national bank like Scotia. But the rule for most people is...no loans.

So that means that every house you see, every car you see, is paid for. In cash.

Now go take a look at the homes and the cars. Drive through San Jose, Costa Rica and see the brand new diesel SUVs that sell for $80,000 USD because they have to add heavy import taxes to the price and tell yourself. Paid for. In cash.

Go look at the sprawling homes on four hundred acre ranches that go for two million and up and remind yourself. Paid for. In Cash.

Now go into the tiny villages where small, simple houses sell for $50,000 or even a little as $20,000 and remind yourself that the people living there make about two dollars an hour. Paid for. In Cash.

The best part about paying for everything and not being in any kind of debt is that when you lose your job, you don't lose your house. The people in Central America do not live with the constant fear of needing to maintain the status quo. Many jobs are seasonal, especially in the tourism industry. And many jobs are a one-time deal. Contract jobs, only they don't work for some big contracting company that keeps them employed and paid. They get a contract to put in a dock and when it's done, it's done. This leaves a lot of down time. It is hard when people don't work and they do run out of money. But they don't lose the roof over their head.

In fact, sometimes guys do a job and then they chill out at home until they have spent all their money and then they go look for another job.

Now we first world people think of that as incredibly irresponsible. But listen to a little story about a conversation I had with a lovely older Costa Rican woman. She was well educated and lived in San Jose, the only real city in Costa Rica and the place where most of the money is made. She was on vacation with her family in the little beach town of Puerto Viejo and I met her floating in the hotel pool. Her English was flawless and she was happy to share about her life, her family, and her culture with me.

"We think you Americans are very selfish," she said.

Keep in mind this was a lovely conversation and no offense was intended by her comment. I was genuinely trying to understand how she saw the world and I was thankful for her honesty.

"You work every day for long hours and you never see your family. You don't play with your children and you never see your grandparents or your cousins. You have all this money and instead of taking time off work to enjoy your life, you spend your money on big houses and cars and furniture. You have all this stuff, but you ignore your family."

In her mind, this was heart breaking. And when she expressed it the way she did, I felt the truth of what she was saying.

We are in debt up to our eye balls. And we run around trying to out-do our neighbors thinking that the guy who dies with the most stuff wins. And we lose out big time. We are on anti-depressants. We don't sleep well. We worry ourselves to the point of disease. According to the Happy Planet Index, as of 2016, Costa Rica is the number one happy place in the world. The US didn't even rank in the top ten. In fact, Nic Marks, creator of The Happy Planet Index said, "The future might not be North America or Western Europe. It might be Latin America!"

Those guys who work for a few weeks and then relax and hang out with friends and family are actually pretty happy. They have simple, but functional homes. They often have cars. They eat well. And they have lots of time to enjoy doing the things they love to do—which usually means hanging out with friends and family, going fishing, hiking in the woods, or working on a project like a new dugout canoe. The sort of things we think we need to work our whole lives and save for. The sort of things we think we can't do until we retire.

What a trap we have fallen into!

So let's go back to idea of poverty.

In my opinion the idea that {poverty = lack of money} no longer seems correct.

I want to break this thought line for a moment to acknowledge there is abject poverty in Latin America. There are conditions that are shocking. There are people who are hungry and literally have nothing. But for some weird reason, even these people seem happier than most

Americans I know.

I do not pretend to have the answers. I am just an observer. And I have lived in poor neighborhoods and on Indian islands. I have washed my clothes by hand and gone without many modern conveniences. I felt I was up for the challenge and I wanted to get up close and personal. I wanted to get to KNOW the local people. And I have found I love them.

Back to the poverty thing.

Can we please re-define that word?

Can we please look at over-all quality of life? Can we please look past the rusted roofs of simple homes and go inside? Can we sit at the table and listen to the conversation? Can we play with the kids and go fishing with the old men? Can we help the mamas cook rice and beans and salad and chicken and get their secret recipes?

Life is beautiful.

61. YOUR EGO IS SHOWING

Ego is that thing that makes you aware of yourself. It makes you feel self-conscience. Maybe you are standing in a room full of people and you feel uncomfortable because you are underdressed, or over-dressed.

That is ego.

It's the thing that makes you focus on yourself instead of what is going on in front of you. Maybe you are in the middle of a conversation and you are thinking of what you want to say next instead of listening to what the other person has to say. That is ego.

To make it simple, another word you can use for ego is *self*.

Think about it for a minute.

Self-conscience.

Conscience of your*self*.

Now try to remember a time when you were completely unaware of your*self*.

You were probably watching a football game or listening to your favorite song. Or maybe you were working on a project like refinishing a piece of furniture or painting a picture. But whatever you were doing, you were so involved in it that you were completely present.

Completely immersed in the thing you were doing.

Ego is fear.

Sometimes it uses words, and sometimes it just uses feelings. It's the thing that makes you feel stupid when you are trying to learn something new.

Imagine you are trying to learn how to ice skate and your legs are all wobbly. If you are out of your ego, you feel the coolness of the air on your face and the slippery feeling of the ice under your feet. Your heart swoons with joy when you slide across the ice and your stomach bubbles up inside you when you lose your balance for just a moment. Your feelings are similar to those you might have if you were on a ride at Disney World.

But if *self* is conscience, you hardly notice the coolness or the exhilarating feeling of sliding. Instead you secretly look around you to see who might be watching. You miss the joy. You miss the ride entirely.

Try this: Go outside and go for a walk. Be aware of your senses. Feel the temperature of the air on your skin. Take a deep breath and smell the air. Look at the color of the sky and at the fine details of your environment. Focus on what you can hear. Are there birds singing?

Become present.

Now let's talk about sitting with a homeless man.

You are in a little island town. It's eleven-thirty at night. There is music blaring off in the distance. Garbage is strewn along the sides of the streets. A few drunk Jamaican boys are hollering at each other. Young, party-loving tourists are raiding the grocery store looking for something to eat. It's raining.

You are sitting under the eaves of the grocery store to stay dry and the young partiers are walking right past you. You are sitting on the cement. The damp cement. You are sitting on the cement and the homeless man is sitting on his cardboard. And the faint smell of that garbage drifts over to you, stronger sometimes depending on the gusts of wind and rain.

Are you uncomfortable? Are you aware of the brief, but strange looks you are getting from the vacationing partiers? Are you aware of the elevated emotions of the yelling drunk Jamaicans? Are you feeling disgusted by the sweet rotting smell of the trash?

The answer would almost have to be yes.

That is our normal reaction. It was mine. I felt all those things. They came to me quickly. Even repeatedly. I am not immune to the ploy of ego.

But if I had given my attention to those things, I would have missed one of the most amazing stories I have ever heard. I would not have listened intently to the man in front of me and I would have found it so difficult to understand his speech that I probably would have walked away. He spoke Creole English and Spanish mixed and he told me stories of pirates and drug running and evil spirits and growing up in Latin America. His story blew me away.

But there is more to this ego thing. And it's the part gentle souls who want to save the world don't like to hear.

Can you envision yourself sitting there, next to the homeless man and listening intently to him and pushing away the outside distractions? I am sure you can. Now look inside your thoughts are see what is there. Are you wondering what you can say to help this man? Do you have a plan to help him and you are wondering when you will get the right break in the conversation to give him your message?

Then you are still *self*-aware.

Your ego is showing.

And he can see it.

However much you may want to help him, he can feel that you have an agenda. Your eyes flit back and forth reading the text that is inside your thoughts and the homeless man sees that he doesn't have your full attention.

So he begins to shut down. He doesn't trust you. You are not there simply because you care. You are not interested in being his friend. You are there because of your own self-interest.

Sounds harsh, I know.

But let the truth of it sink in.

Try to put yourself in the homeless man's shoes. He doesn't have many friends. Yes, people throw him a few coins or even take him into a restaurant and buy him something to eat. But he can feel their pity. He is thankful for what he has received, but he has to endure barely veiled disgust to receive it. Try to imagine how you might feel if you knew someone was only taking you out to eat because they were appalled at your life and felt bad for you.

In order to really love, you have to get past your own agenda. You have to forget your*self* and become genuinely interested in the one in front of you. You have to let go of fear. Fear keeps you defensive. It separates you from the person standing in front of you. It isn't until you lose consciousness of your*self* that you can truly connect. And that authentic connection is the most beautiful gift you can give that person.

I know if you are reading this, you DO have a heart to help. And if you persevere, the material things will fall into place. By getting to know that homeless man, you will discover what his real needs are. And ideally, you will be able to help him come up with some long term solutions. But what is more precious than anything. What he needs more than your pity or your concern or even the dollars in your pocket...is a friend.

62. THE POWER TO CHANGE

Why do we manifest the things we do? I pray for the perfect mate and synchronicity arrives at my doorstep all tall dark and handsome. Signs everywhere confirm this is the right one, my soul mate. The stars sing together and the flowers bloom and every car license plate I drive by bears the name of my new found love.

And slowly I discover this person is out to kill me.

Why? I asked. I prayed. I followed the signs. Everything seemed so perfect.

It was.

I got exactly what I asked for.

Our deep inner desires pull from the far-flung reaches of the universe. They gather the things we ask for. So why do we end up with things that hurt us?

Because that is what we asked for.

Look deep inside yourself. Do you have a controlling lover? Then somewhere down in the depths of your soul, you want to be controlled.

Now I am sure by this time, you must be angry at me or getting ready to throw my words aside. But please don't, because my desire is for your healing. This information is powerful. It can set you free. If you can put aside your feeling of offense and unemotionally take a look at what you are attracting, you can find the root of your pain. And if you can find the root of it, then you can discover the lie you are believing and you can re-program your brain.

You will attract what you long for. So look at what you are attracting to discover what you really desire.

Let's go back to the example of the person who attracts a controlling mate. What power to realize they want to be controlled! Now the question is why? What happened long ago? What do they believe about themselves? What defense mechanism do they no longer need?

Perhaps they felt they needed to be punished. Perhaps their sister died in a car accident when they were three and they tried to tell her not to get in the car but she didn't listen. Perhaps they felt the death was their fault and now they desire to pay the piper and that equates to eternal punishment.

It sounds sick, I know. But we do these things to ourselves, most of the time without even realizing it. And we need to get free.

Take time to sit with the reality of your life, the things that keep coming to you and do not serve you. Ask yourself what common thread you see. If you can identify the common thread, you can discover what the deep, dark resources of your soul desires. This is where healing begins.

When you identify the darkness inside you, hold it up to the light. Is it truth? It never is. Even if you have done something terrible and you feel you can never be forgiven. Forgiveness is possible. Run to Heaven. Pour out your pain and find the sweet balm of love that flows from All Goodness and washes away your guilt and your stain.

Truth sets us free.

It sets us free from a lifetime of self-abuse. The Truth of the universe, the Grid that holds all things together is Love. Love heals. Love forgives. Love believes.

Allow Love to shed its light on the lies you laid hold of. And I tell you the truth, Love will set you free.

ABOUT THE AUTHOR

Laura LaBrie

Founder of Poverty Project International. Aimless wanderer. Photographer of the beauty in the poor places. Documenter of the underbelly of life. Teacher. Mentor. Wearer of flip-flops. Cave diver. Musician. Artist. And most importantly, mom.
www.povertyprojectinternational.com